The Merchant of Venice by William Shakespeare

The life of William Shakespeare, arguably the most significant figure in the Western literary canon, is relatively unknown.

Shakespeare was born in Stratford-upon-Avon in 1565, possibly on the 23rd April, St. George's Day, and baptised there on 26th April.

Little is known of his education and the first firm facts to his life relate to his marriage, aged 18, to Anne Hathaway, who was 26 and from the nearby village of Shottery. Anne gave birth to their first son six months later.

Shakespeare's first play, The Comedy of Errors began a procession of real heavyweights that were to emanate from his pen in a career of just over twenty years in which 37 plays were written and his reputation forever established.

This early skill was recognised by many and by 1594 the Lord Chamberlain's Men were performing his works. With the advantage of Shakespeare's progressive writing they rapidly became London's leading company of players, affording him more exposure and, following the death of Queen Elizabeth in 1603, a royal patent by the new king, James I, at which point they changed their name to the King's Men.

By 1598, and despite efforts to pirate his work, Shakespeare's name was well known and had become a selling point in its own right on title pages.

No plays are attributed to Shakespeare after 1613, and the last few plays he wrote before this time were in collaboration with other writers, one of whom is likely to be John Fletcher who succeeded him as the house playwright for the King's Men.

William Shakespeare died two months later on April 23rd, 1616, survived by his wife, two daughters and a legacy of writing that none have since yet eclipsed.

Index of Contents

DRAMATIS PERSONAE
ACT I
Scene I - Venice. A Street.
Scene II - Venice. A Public Place.
ACT II
Scene I - Belmont. A Room in Portia's House.
Scene II - Venice. A Street.
Scene III: The Same. A Room in Shylock's House.
Scene IV: The Same. A Street.
Scene V: The Same. Before Shylock's House.
Scene VI: The Same.
Scene VII: Belmont. A Room in Portia's House.
Scene VIII: Venice. A Street.
Scene IX: Belmont. A Room in Portia's House.
ACT III

Scene I - Venice. A Street.
Scene II - Belmont. A Room in Portia's House.
Scene III - Venice. A Street.
Scene IV - Belmont. A Room in Portia's House.
Scene V - The Same. A Garden.
ACT IV
Scene I - Venice. A Court of Justice.
Scene II - The Same. A Street.
ACT V
Scene I - Belmont. Avenue to Portia's House.
William Shakespeare – A Short Biography
William Shakespeare – A Concise Bibliography
Shakespeare; or, the Poet by Ralph Waldo Emerson
William Shakespeare – A Tribute in Verse

DRAMATIS PERSONAE

DUKE OF VENICE.
PRINCE OF MOROCCO & PRINCE OF ARRAGON, Suitors to Portia.
ANTONIO, a Merchant of Venice.
BASSANIO, his Friend.
GRATIANO, SALANIO, & SALARINO: Friends to Antonio and Bassanio.
LORENZO, in love with Jessica.
SHYLOCK, a rich Jew.
TUBAL, a Jew, his Friend.
LAUNCELOT GOBBO, a Clown, Servant to Shylock.
OLD GOBBO, Father to Launcelot.
LEONARDO, Servant to Bassanio.
BALTHAZAR & STEPHANO: Servants to Portia.

PORTIA, a rich Heiress.
NERISSA, her Waiting-maid.
JESSICA, Daughter to Shylock.
Magnificoes of Venice, Officers of the Court of Justice, Gaoler, Servants to Portia, and other Attendants.

SCENE.—Partly at Venice, and partly at Belmont, the seat of Portia, on the Continent.

ACT I

SCENE I. Venice. A Street.

Enter ANTONIO, SALARINO, and SALANIO

ANTONIO

In sooth, I know not why I am so sad:
It wearies me; you say it wearies you;
But how I caught it, found it, or came by it,
What stuff 'tis made of, whereof it is born,
I am to learn;
And such a want-wit sadness makes of me,
That I have much ado to know myself.

SALARINO
Your mind is tossing on the ocean;
There, where your argosies with portly sail,
Like signiors and rich burghers on the flood,
Or, as it were, the pageants of the sea,
Do overpeer the petty traffickers,
That curtsy to them, do them reverence,
As they fly by them with their woven wings.

SALANIO
Believe me, sir, had I such venture forth,
The better part of my affections would
Be with my hopes abroad. I should be still
Plucking the grass, to know where sits the wind,
Peering in maps for ports and piers and roads;
And every object that might make me fear
Misfortune to my ventures, out of doubt
Would make me sad.

SALARINO
My wind cooling my broth
Would blow me to an ague, when I thought
What harm a wind too great at sea might do.
I should not see the sandy hour-glass run,
But I should think of shallows and of flats,
And see my wealthy Andrew dock'd in sand,
Vailing her high-top lower than her ribs
To kiss her burial. Should I go to church
And see the holy edifice of stone,
And not bethink me straight of dangerous rocks,
Which touching but my gentle vessel's side,
Would scatter all her spices on the stream,
Enrobe the roaring waters with my silks,
And, in a word, but even now worth this,
And now worth nothing? Shall I have the thought
To think on this, and shall I lack the thought
That such a thing bechanced would make me sad?
But tell not me; I know, Antonio
Is sad to think upon his merchandise.

ANTONIO
Believe me, no: I thank my fortune for it,
My ventures are not in one bottom trusted,

Nor to one place; nor is my whole estate
Upon the fortune of this present year:
Therefore my merchandise makes me not sad.

SALARINO
Why, then you are in love.

ANTONIO
Fie, fie!

SALARINO
Not in love neither? Then let us say you are sad,
Because you are not merry: and 'twere as easy
For you to laugh and leap and say you are merry,
Because you are not sad. Now, by two-headed Janus,
Nature hath framed strange fellows in her time:
Some that will evermore peep through their eyes
And laugh like parrots at a bag-piper,
And other of such vinegar aspect
That they'll not show their teeth in way of smile,
Though Nestor swear the jest be laughable.

Enter BASSANIO, LORENZO, and GRATIANO

SALANIO
Here comes Bassanio, your most noble kinsman,
Gratiano and Lorenzo. Fare ye well:
We leave you now with better company.

SALARINO
I would have stay'd till I had made you merry,
If worthier friends had not prevented me.

ANTONIO
Your worth is very dear in my regard.
I take it, your own business calls on you
And you embrace the occasion to depart.

SALARINO
Good morrow, my good lords.

BASSANIO
Good signiors both, when shall we laugh? say, when?
You grow exceeding strange: must it be so?

SALARINO
We'll make our leisures to attend on yours.

Exeunt SALARINO and SALANIO

LORENZO

My Lord Bassanio, since you have found Antonio,
We two will leave you: but at dinner-time,
I pray you, have in mind where we must meet.

BASSANIO
I will not fail you.

GRATIANO
You look not well, Signior Antonio;
You have too much respect upon the world:
They lose it that do buy it with much care:
Believe me, you are marvellously changed.

ANTONIO
I hold the world but as the world, Gratiano;
A stage where every man must play a part,
And mine a sad one.

GRATIANO
Let me play the fool:
With mirth and laughter let old wrinkles come,
And let my liver rather heat with wine
Than my heart cool with mortifying groans.
Why should a man, whose blood is warm within,
Sit like his grandsire cut in alabaster?
Sleep when he wakes and creep into the jaundice
By being peevish? I tell thee what, Antonio—
I love thee, and it is my love that speaks—
There are a sort of men whose visages
Do cream and mantle like a standing pond,
And do a wilful stillness entertain,
With purpose to be dress'd in an opinion
Of wisdom, gravity, profound conceit,
As who should say 'I am Sir Oracle,
And when I ope my lips let no dog bark!'
O my Antonio, I do know of these
That therefore only are reputed wise
For saying nothing; when, I am very sure,
If they should speak, would almost damn those ears,
Which, hearing them, would call their brothers fools.
I'll tell thee more of this another time:
But fish not, with this melancholy bait,
For this fool gudgeon, this opinion.
Come, good Lorenzo. Fare ye well awhile:
I'll end my exhortation after dinner.

LORENZO
Well, we will leave you then till dinner-time:
I must be one of these same dumb wise men,
For Gratiano never lets me speak.

GRATIANO
Well, keep me company but two years moe,
Thou shalt not know the sound of thine own tongue.

ANTONIO
Farewell: I'll grow a talker for this gear.

GRATIANO
Thanks, i' faith, for silence is only commendable
In a neat's tongue dried and a maid not vendible.

Exeunt GRATIANO and LORENZO

ANTONIO
Is that any thing now?

BASSANIO
Gratiano speaks an infinite deal of nothing, more than any man in all Venice. His reasons are as two grains of wheat hid in two bushels of chaff: you shall seek all day ere you find them, and when you have them, they are not worth the search.

ANTONIO
Well, tell me now what lady is the same
To whom you swore a secret pilgrimage,
That you to-day promised to tell me of?

BASSANIO
'Tis not unknown to you, Antonio,
How much I have disabled mine estate,
By something showing a more swelling port
Than my faint means would grant continuance:
Nor do I now make moan to be abridged
From such a noble rate; but my chief care
Is to come fairly off from the great debts
Wherein my time something too prodigal
Hath left me gaged. To you, Antonio,
I owe the most, in money and in love,
And from your love I have a warranty
To unburden all my plots and purposes
How to get clear of all the debts I owe.

ANTONIO
I pray you, good Bassanio, let me know it;
And if it stand, as you yourself still do,
Within the eye of honour, be assured,
My purse, my person, my extremest means,
Lie all unlock'd to your occasions.

BASSANIO
In my school-days, when I had lost one shaft,
I shot his fellow of the self-same flight

The self-same way with more advised watch,
To find the other forth, and by adventuring both
I oft found both: I urge this childhood proof,
Because what follows is pure innocence.
I owe you much, and, like a wilful youth,
That which I owe is lost; but if you please
To shoot another arrow that self way
Which you did shoot the first, I do not doubt,
As I will watch the aim, or to find both
Or bring your latter hazard back again
And thankfully rest debtor for the first.

ANTONIO
You know me well, and herein spend but time
To wind about my love with circumstance;
And out of doubt you do me now more wrong
In making question of my uttermost
Than if you had made waste of all I have:
Then do but say to me what I should do
That in your knowledge may by me be done,
And I am prest unto it: therefore, speak.

BASSANIO
In Belmont is a lady richly left;
And she is fair, and, fairer than that word,
Of wondrous virtues: sometimes from her eyes
I did receive fair speechless messages:
Her name is Portia, nothing undervalued
To Cato's daughter, Brutus' Portia:
Nor is the wide world ignorant of her worth,
For the four winds blow in from every coast
Renowned suitors, and her sunny locks
Hang on her temples like a golden fleece;
Which makes her seat of Belmont Colchos' strand,
And many Jasons come in quest of her.
O my Antonio, had I but the means
To hold a rival place with one of them,
I have a mind presages me such thrift,
That I should questionless be fortunate!

ANTONIO
Thou know'st that all my fortunes are at sea;
Neither have I money nor commodity
To raise a present sum: therefore go forth;
Try what my credit can in Venice do:
That shall be rack'd, even to the uttermost,
To furnish thee to Belmont, to fair Portia.
Go, presently inquire, and so will I,
Where money is, and I no question make
To have it of my trust or for my sake.

Exeunt

SCENE II: Belmont. A Room in Portia's House.

Enter PORTIA and NERISSA

PORTIA
By my troth, Nerissa, my little body is aweary of this great world.

NERISSA
You would be, sweet madam, if your miseries were in the same abundance as your good fortunes are: and yet, for aught I see, they are as sick that surfeit with too much as they that starve with nothing. It is no mean happiness therefore, to be seated in the mean: superfluity comes sooner by white hairs, but competency lives longer.

PORTIA
Good sentences and well pronounced.

NERISSA
They would be better, if well followed.

PORTIA
If to do were as easy as to know what were good to do, chapels had been churches and poor men's cottages princes' palaces. It is a good divine that follows his own instructions: I can easier teach twenty what were good to be done, than be one of the twenty to follow mine own teaching. The brain may devise laws for the blood, but a hot temper leaps o'er a cold decree: such a hare is madness the youth, to skip o'er the meshes of good counsel the cripple. But this reasoning is not in the fashion to choose me a husband. O me, the word 'choose!' I may neither choose whom I would nor refuse whom I dislike; so is the will of a living daughter curbed by the will of a dead father. Is it not hard, Nerissa, that I cannot choose one nor refuse none?

NERISSA
Your father was ever virtuous; and holy men at their death have good inspirations: therefore the lottery, that he hath devised in these three chests of gold, silver and lead, whereof who chooses his meaning chooses you, will, no doubt, never be chosen by any rightly but one who shall rightly love. But what warmth is there in your affection towards any of these princely suitors that are already come?

PORTIA
I pray thee, over-name them; and as thou namest them, I will describe them; and, according to my description, level at my affection.

NERISSA
First, there is the Neapolitan prince.

PORTIA
Ay, that's a colt indeed, for he doth nothing but talk of his horse; and he makes it a great appropriation to his own good parts, that he can shoe him himself. I am much afeard my lady his mother played false with a smith.

NERISSA

Then there is the County Palatine.

PORTIA

He doth nothing but frown, as who should say 'If you will not have me, choose:' he hears merry tales and smiles not: I fear he will prove the weeping philosopher when he grows old, being so full of unmannerly sadness in his youth. I had rather be married to a death's-head with a bone in his mouth than to either of these. God defend me from these two!

NERISSA

How say you by the French lord, Monsieur Le Bon?

PORTIA

God made him, and therefore let him pass for a man. In truth, I know it is a sin to be a mocker: but, he! why, he hath a horse better than the Neapolitan's, a better bad habit of frowning than the Count Palatine; he is every man in no man; if a throstle sing, he falls straight a capering: he will fence with his own shadow: if I should marry him, I should marry twenty husbands. If he would despise me I would forgive him, for if he love me to madness, I shall never requite him.

NERISSA

What say you, then, to Falconbridge, the young baron of England?

PORTIA

You know I say nothing to him, for he understands not me, nor I him: he hath neither Latin, French, nor Italian, and you will come into the court and swear that I have a poor pennyworth in the English. He is a proper man's picture, but, alas, who can converse with a dumb-show? How oddly he is suited! I think he bought his doublet in Italy, his round hose in France, his bonnet in Germany and his behavior every where.

NERISSA

What think you of the Scottish lord, his neighbour?

PORTIA

That he hath a neighbourly charity in him, for he borrowed a box of the ear of the Englishman and swore he would pay him again when he was able: I think the Frenchman became his surety and sealed under for another.

NERISSA

How like you the young German, the Duke of Saxony's nephew?

PORTIA

Very vilely in the morning, when he is sober, and most vilely in the afternoon, when he is drunk: when he is best, he is a little worse than a man, and when he is worst, he is little better than a beast: and the worst fall that ever fell, I hope I shall make shift to go without him.

NERISSA

If he should offer to choose, and choose the right casket, you should refuse to perform your father's will, if you should refuse to accept him.

PORTIA

Therefore, for fear of the worst, I pray thee, set a deep glass of rhenish wine on the contrary casket, for if the devil be within and that temptation without, I know he will choose it. I will do anything, Nerissa, ere I'll be married to a sponge.

NERISSA
You need not fear, lady, the having any of these lords: they have acquainted me with their determinations; which is, indeed, to return to their home and to trouble you with no more suit, unless you may be won by some other sort than your father's imposition depending on the caskets.

PORTIA
If I live to be as old as Sibylla, I will die as chaste as Diana, unless I be obtained by the manner of my father's will. I am glad this parcel of wooers are so reasonable, for there is not one among them but I dote on his very absence, and I pray God grant them a fair departure.

NERISSA
Do you not remember, lady, in your father's time, a Venetian, a scholar and a soldier, that came hither in company of the Marquis of Montferrat?

PORTIA
Yes, yes, it was Bassanio; as I think, he was so called.

NERISSA
True, madam: he, of all the men that ever my foolish eyes looked upon, was the best deserving a fair lady.

PORTIA
I remember him well, and I remember him worthy of thy praise.

Enter a SERVING-MAN

How now! what news?

SERVANT
The four strangers seek for you, madam, to take their leave: and there is a forerunner come from a fifth, the Prince of Morocco, who brings word the prince his master will be here to-night.

PORTIA
If I could bid the fifth welcome with so good a heart as I can bid the other four farewell, I should be glad of his approach: if he have the condition of a saint and the complexion of a devil, I had rather he should shrive me than wive me. Come, Nerissa. Sirrah, go before. Whiles we shut the gates upon one wooer, another knocks at the door.

Exeunt

SCENE III. Venice. A Public Place.

Enter BASSANIO and SHYLOCK

SHYLOCK

Three thousand ducats; well.

BASSANIO
Ay, sir, for three months.

SHYLOCK
For three months; well.

BASSANIO
For the which, as I told you, Antonio shall be bound.

SHYLOCK
Antonio shall become bound; well.

BASSANIO
May you stead me? will you pleasure me? shall I know your answer?

SHYLOCK
Three thousand ducats for three months and Antonio bound.

BASSANIO
Your answer to that.

SHYLOCK
Antonio is a good man.

BASSANIO
Have you heard any imputation to the contrary?

SHYLOCK
Oh, no, no, no, no: my meaning in saying he is a good man is to have you understand me that he is sufficient. Yet his means are in supposition: he hath an argosy bound to Tripolis, another to the Indies; I understand moreover, upon the Rialto, he hath a third at Mexico, a fourth for England, and other ventures he hath, squandered abroad. But ships are but boards, sailors but men: there be land-rats and water-rats, water-thieves and land-thieves, I mean pirates, and then there is the peril of waters, winds and rocks. The man is, notwithstanding, sufficient. Three thousand ducats; I think I may take his bond.

BASSANIO
Be assured you may.

SHYLOCK
I will be assured I may; and, that I may be assured, I will bethink me. May I speak with Antonio?

BASSANIO
If it please you to dine with us.

SHYLOCK
Yes, to smell pork; to eat of the habitation which your prophet the Nazarite conjured the devil into. I will buy with you, sell with you, talk with you, walk with you, and so following, but I will not eat with you, drink with you, nor pray with you. What news on the Rialto? Who is he comes here?

Enter ANTONIO

BASSANIO
This is Signior Antonio.

SHYLOCK
[Aside] How like a fawning publican he looks!
I hate him for he is a Christian,
But more for that in low simplicity
He lends out money gratis and brings down
The rate of usance here with us in Venice.
If I can catch him once upon the hip,
I will feed fat the ancient grudge I bear him.
He hates our sacred nation, and he rails,
Even there where merchants most do congregate,
On me, my bargains and my well-won thrift,
Which he calls interest. Cursed be my tribe,
If I forgive him!

BASSANIO
Shylock, do you hear?

SHYLOCK
I am debating of my present store,
And, by the near guess of my memory,
I cannot instantly raise up the gross
Of full three thousand ducats. What of that?
Tubal, a wealthy Hebrew of my tribe,
Will furnish me. But soft! how many months
Do you desire?

To ANTONIO

Rest you fair, good signior;
Your worship was the last man in our mouths.

ANTONIO
Shylock, although I neither lend nor borrow
By taking nor by giving of excess,
Yet, to supply the ripe wants of my friend,
I'll break a custom. Is he yet possess'd
How much ye would?

SHYLOCK
Ay, ay, three thousand ducats.

ANTONIO
And for three months.

SHYLOCK

I had forgot; three months; you told me so.
Well then, your bond; and let me see; but hear you;
Methought you said you neither lend nor borrow
Upon advantage.

ANTONIO
I do never use it.

SHYLOCK
When Jacob grazed his uncle Laban's sheep—
This Jacob from our holy Abram was,
As his wise mother wrought in his behalf,
The third possessor; ay, he was the third—

ANTONIO
And what of him? did he take interest?

SHYLOCK
No, not take interest, not, as you would say,
Directly interest: mark what Jacob did.
When Laban and himself were compromised
That all the eanlings which were streak'd and pied
Should fall as Jacob's hire, the ewes, being rank,
In the end of autumn turned to the rams,
And, when the work of generation was
Between these woolly breeders in the act,
The skilful shepherd peel'd me certain wands,
And, in the doing of the deed of kind,
He stuck them up before the fulsome ewes,
Who then conceiving did in eaning time
Fall parti-colour'd lambs, and those were Jacob's.
This was a way to thrive, and he was blest:
And thrift is blessing, if men steal it not.

ANTONIO
This was a venture, sir, that Jacob served for;
A thing not in his power to bring to pass,
But sway'd and fashion'd by the hand of heaven.
Was this inserted to make interest good?
Or is your gold and silver ewes and rams?

SHYLOCK
I cannot tell; I make it breed as fast:
But note me, signior.

ANTONIO
Mark you this, Bassanio,
The devil can cite Scripture for his purpose.
An evil soul producing holy witness
Is like a villain with a smiling cheek,

A goodly apple rotten at the heart:
O, what a goodly outside falsehood hath!

SHYLOCK
Three thousand ducats; 'tis a good round sum.
Three months from twelve; then, let me see; the rate—

ANTONIO
Well, Shylock, shall we be beholding to you?

SHYLOCK
Signior Antonio, many a time and oft
In the Rialto you have rated me
About my moneys and my usances:
Still have I borne it with a patient shrug,
For sufferance is the badge of all our tribe.
You call me misbeliever, cut-throat dog,
And spit upon my Jewish gaberdine,
And all for use of that which is mine own.
Well then, it now appears you need my help:
Go to, then; you come to me, and you say
'Shylock, we would have moneys:' you say so;
You, that did void your rheum upon my beard
And foot me as you spurn a stranger cur
Over your threshold: moneys is your suit
What should I say to you? Should I not say
'Hath a dog money? is it possible
A cur can lend three thousand ducats?' Or
Shall I bend low and in a bondman's key,
With bated breath and whispering humbleness, Say this;
'Fair sir, you spit on me on Wednesday last;
You spurn'd me such a day; another time
You call'd me dog; and for these courtesies
I'll lend you thus much moneys'?

ANTONIO
I am as like to call thee so again,
To spit on thee again, to spurn thee too.
If thou wilt lend this money, lend it not
As to thy friends; for when did friendship take
A breed for barren metal of his friend?
But lend it rather to thine enemy,
Who, if he break, thou mayst with better face
Exact the penalty.

SHYLOCK
Why, look you, how you storm!
I would be friends with you and have your love,
Forget the shames that you have stain'd me with,
Supply your present wants and take no doit

Of usance for my moneys, and you'll not hear me:
This is kind I offer.

BASSANIO
This were kindness.

SHYLOCK
This kindness will I show.
Go with me to a notary, seal me there
Your single bond; and, in a merry sport,
If you repay me not on such a day,
In such a place, such sum or sums as are
Express'd in the condition, let the forfeit
Be nominated for an equal pound
Of your fair flesh, to be cut off and taken
In what part of your body pleaseth me.

ANTONIO
Content, i' faith: I'll seal to such a bond
And say there is much kindness in the Jew.

BASSANIO
You shall not seal to such a bond for me:
I'll rather dwell in my necessity.

ANTONIO
Why, fear not, man; I will not forfeit it:
Within these two months, that's a month before
This bond expires, I do expect return
Of thrice three times the value of this bond.

SHYLOCK
O father Abram, what these Christians are,
Whose own hard dealings teaches them suspect
The thoughts of others! Pray you, tell me this;
If he should break his day, what should I gain
By the exaction of the forfeiture?
A pound of man's flesh taken from a man
Is not so estimable, profitable neither,
As flesh of muttons, beefs, or goats. I say,
To buy his favour, I extend this friendship:
If he will take it, so; if not, adieu;
And, for my love, I pray you wrong me not.

ANTONIO
Yes Shylock, I will seal unto this bond.

SHYLOCK
Then meet me forthwith at the notary's;
Give him direction for this merry bond,
And I will go and purse the ducats straight,

See to my house, left in the fearful guard
Of an unthrifty knave, and presently
I will be with you.

ANTONIO
Hie thee, gentle Jew.

Exit Shylock

The Hebrew will turn Christian: he grows kind.

BASSANIO
I like not fair terms and a villain's mind.

ANTONIO
Come on: in this there can be no dismay;
My ships come home a month before the day.

Exeunt

ACT II

SCENE I. Belmont. A Room in Portia's House.

Flourish of cornets. Enter the PRINCE OF MOROCCO and his train; PORTIA, NERISSA, and others Attending

MOROCCO
Mislike me not for my complexion,
The shadow'd livery of the burnish'd sun,
To whom I am a neighbour and near bred.
Bring me the fairest creature northward born,
Where Phoebus' fire scarce thaws the icicles,
And let us make incision for your love,
To prove whose blood is reddest, his or mine.
I tell thee, lady, this aspect of mine
Hath fear'd the valiant: by my love I swear
The best-regarded virgins of our clime
Have loved it too: I would not change this hue,
Except to steal your thoughts, my gentle queen.

PORTIA
In terms of choice I am not solely led
By nice direction of a maiden's eyes;
Besides, the lottery of my destiny
Bars me the right of voluntary choosing:
But if my father had not scanted me
And hedged me by his wit, to yield myself

His wife who wins me by that means I told you,
Yourself, renowned prince, then stood as fair
As any comer I have look'd on yet
For my affection.

MOROCCO
Even for that I thank you:
Therefore, I pray you, lead me to the caskets
To try my fortune. By this scimitar
That slew the Sophy and a Persian prince
That won three fields of Sultan Solyman,
I would outstare the sternest eyes that look,
Outbrave the heart most daring on the earth,
Pluck the young sucking cubs from the she-bear,
Yea, mock the lion when he roars for prey,
To win thee, lady. But, alas the while!
If Hercules and Lichas play at dice
Which is the better man, the greater throw
May turn by fortune from the weaker hand:
So is Alcides beaten by his page;
And so may I, blind fortune leading me,
Miss that which one unworthier may attain,
And die with grieving.

PORTIA
You must take your chance,
And either not attempt to choose at all
Or swear before you choose, if you choose wrong
Never to speak to lady afterward
In way of marriage: therefore be advised.

MOROCCO
Nor will not. Come, bring me unto my chance.

PORTIA
First, forward to the temple: after dinner
Your hazard shall be made.

MOROCCO
Good fortune then!
To make me blest or cursed'st among men.

Cornets, and exeunt

SCENE II. Venice. A Street.

Enter LAUNCELOT

LAUNCELOT

Certainly my conscience will serve me to run from this Jew my master. The fiend is at mine elbow and tempts me saying to me 'Gobbo, Launcelot Gobbo, good Launcelot,' or 'good Gobbo,' or good Launcelot Gobbo, use your legs, take the start, run away. My conscience says 'No; take heed,' honest Launcelot; take heed, honest Gobbo, or, as aforesaid, 'honest Launcelot Gobbo; do not run; scorn running with thy heels.' Well, the most courageous fiend bids me pack: 'Via!' says the fiend; 'away!' says the fiend; 'for the heavens, rouse up a brave mind,' says the fiend, 'and run.' Well, my conscience, hanging about the neck of my heart, says very wisely to me 'My honest friend Launcelot, being an honest man's son,' or rather an honest woman's son; for, indeed, my father did something smack, something grow to, he had a kind of taste; well, my conscience says 'Launcelot, budge not.' 'Budge,' says the fiend. 'Budge not,' says my conscience. 'Conscience,' say I, 'you counsel well;' ' Fiend,' say I, 'you counsel well:' to be ruled by my conscience, I should stay with the Jew my master, who, God bless the mark, is a kind of devil; and, to run away from the Jew, I should be ruled by the fiend, who, saving your reverence, is the devil himself. Certainly the Jew is the very devil incarnal; and, in my conscience, my conscience is but a kind of hard conscience, to offer to counsel me to stay with the Jew. The fiend gives the more friendly counsel: I will run, fiend; my heels are at your command; I will run.

Enter Old GOBBO, with a basket

GOBBO
Master young man, you, I pray you, which is the way to master Jew's?

LAUNCELOT
[Aside] O heavens, this is my true-begotten father! who, being more than sand-blind, high-gravel blind, knows me not: I will try confusions with him.

GOBBO
Master young gentleman, I pray you, which is the way to master Jew's?

LAUNCELOT
Turn up on your right hand at the next turning, but, at the next turning of all, on your left; marry, at the very next turning, turn of no hand, but turn down indirectly to the Jew's house.

GOBBO
By God's sonties, 'twill be a hard way to hit. Can you tell me whether one Launcelot, that dwells with him, dwell with him or no?

LAUNCELOT
Talk you of young Master Launcelot?
Aside
Mark me now; now will I raise the waters. Talk you of young Master Launcelot?

GOBBO
No master, sir, but a poor man's son: his father, though I say it, is an honest exceeding poor man and, God be thanked, well to live.

LAUNCELOT
Well, let his father be what a' will, we talk of young Master Launcelot.

GOBBO
Your worship's friend and Launcelot, sir.

LAUNCELOT
But I pray you, ergo, old man, ergo, I beseech you, talk you of young Master Launcelot?

GOBBO
Of Launcelot, an't please your mastership.

LAUNCELOT
Ergo, Master Launcelot. Talk not of Master Launcelot, father; for the young gentleman, according to Fates and Destinies and such odd sayings, the Sisters Three and such branches of learning, is indeed deceased, or, as you would say in plain terms, gone to heaven.

GOBBO
Marry, God forbid! the boy was the very staff of my age, my very prop.

LAUNCELOT
Do I look like a cudgel or a hovel-post, a staff or a prop? Do you know me, father?

GOBBO
Alack the day, I know you not, young gentleman: but, I pray you, tell me, is my boy, God rest his soul, alive or dead?

LAUNCELOT
Do you not know me, father?

GOBBO
Alack, sir, I am sand-blind; I know you not.

LAUNCELOT
Nay, indeed, if you had your eyes, you might fail of the knowing me: it is a wise father that knows his own child. Well, old man, I will tell you news of your son: give me your blessing: truth will come to light; murder cannot be hid long; a man's son may, but at the length truth will out.

GOBBO
Pray you, sir, stand up: I am sure you are not Launcelot, my boy.

LAUNCELOT
Pray you, let's have no more fooling about it, but give me your blessing: I am Launcelot, your boy that was, your son that is, your child that shall be.

GOBBO
I cannot think you are my son.

LAUNCELOT
I know not what I shall think of that: but I am Launcelot, the Jew's man, and I am sure Margery your wife is my mother.

GOBBO
Her name is Margery, indeed: I'll be sworn, if thou be Launcelot, thou art mine own flesh and blood. Lord worshipped might he be! what a beard hast thou got! thou hast got more hair on thy chin than Dobbin my fill-horse has on his tail.

LAUNCELOT

It should seem, then, that Dobbin's tail grows backward: I am sure he had more hair of his tail than I have of my face when I last saw him.

GOBBO

Lord, how art thou changed! How dost thou and thy master agree? I have brought him a present. How 'gree you now?

LAUNCELOT

Well, well: but, for mine own part, as I have set up my rest to run away, so I will not rest till I have run some ground. My master's a very Jew: give him a present! give him a halter: I am famished in his service; you may tell every finger I have with my ribs. Father, I am glad you are come: give me your present to one Master Bassanio, who, indeed, gives rare new liveries: if I serve not him, I will run as far as God has any ground. O rare fortune! here comes the man: to him, father; for I am a Jew, if I serve the Jew any longer.

Enter BASSANIO, with LEONARDO and other followers

BASSANIO

You may do so; but let it be so hasted that supper be ready at the farthest by five of the clock. See these letters delivered; put the liveries to making, and desire Gratiano to come anon to my lodging.

Exit a SERVANT

LAUNCELOT

To him, father.

GOBBO

God bless your worship!

BASSANIO

Gramercy! wouldst thou aught with me?

GOBBO

Here's my son, sir, a poor boy,—

LAUNCELOT

Not a poor boy, sir, but the rich Jew's man; that would, sir, as my father shall specify—

GOBBO

He hath a great infection, sir, as one would say, to serve—

LAUNCELOT

Indeed, the short and the long is, I serve the Jew, and have a desire, as my father shall specify—

GOBBO

His master and he, saving your worship's reverence, are scarce cater-cousins—

LAUNCELOT

To be brief, the very truth is that the Jew, having done me wrong, doth cause me, as my father, being, I hope, an old man, shall frutify unto you—

GOBBO
I have here a dish of doves that I would bestow upon your worship, and my suit is—

LAUNCELOT
In very brief, the suit is impertinent to myself, as your worship shall know by this honest old man; and, though I say it, though old man, yet poor man, my father.

BASSANIO
One speak for both. What would you?

LAUNCELOT
Serve you, sir.

GOBBO
That is the very defect of the matter, sir.

BASSANIO
I know thee well; thou hast obtain'd thy suit:
Shylock thy master spoke with me this day,
And hath preferr'd thee, if it be preferment
To leave a rich Jew's service, to become
The follower of so poor a gentleman.

LAUNCELOT
The old proverb is very well parted between my master Shylock and you, sir: you have the grace of God, sir, and he hath enough.

BASSANIO
Thou speak'st it well. Go, father, with thy son.
Take leave of thy old master and inquire
My lodging out. Give him a livery
More guarded than his fellows': see it done.

LAUNCELOT
Father, in. I cannot get a service, no; I have ne'er a tongue in my head. Well, if any man in Italy have a fairer table which doth offer to swear upon a book, I shall have good fortune. Go to, here's a simple line of life: here's a small trifle of wives: alas, fifteen wives is nothing! Eleven widows and nine maids is a simple coming-in for one man: and then to 'scape drowning thrice, and to be in peril of my life with the edge of a feather-bed; here are simple scapes. Well, if Fortune be a woman, she's a good wench for this gear. Father, come; I'll take my leave of the Jew in the twinkling of an eye.

Exeunt LAUNCELOT and OLD GOBBO

BASSANIO
I pray thee, good Leonardo, think on this:
These things being bought and orderly bestow'd,
Return in haste, for I do feast to-night
My best-esteem'd acquaintance: hie thee, go.

LEONARDO
My best endeavours shall be done herein.

Enter GRATIANO

GRATIANO
Where is your master?

LEONARDO
Yonder, sir, he walks.

Exit

GRATIANO
Signior Bassanio!

BASSANIO
Gratiano!

GRATIANO
I have a suit to you.

BASSANIO
You have obtain'd it.

GRATIANO
You must not deny me: I must go with you to Belmont.

BASSANIO
Why then you must. But hear thee, Gratiano;
Thou art too wild, too rude and bold of voice;
Parts that become thee happily enough
And in such eyes as ours appear not faults;
But where thou art not known, why, there they show
Something too liberal. Pray thee, take pain
To allay with some cold drops of modesty
Thy skipping spirit, lest through thy wild behavior
I be misconstrued in the place I go to,
And lose my hopes.

GRATIANO
Signior Bassanio, hear me:
If I do not put on a sober habit,
Talk with respect and swear but now and then,
Wear prayer-books in my pocket, look demurely,
Nay more, while grace is saying, hood mine eyes
Thus with my hat, and sigh and say 'amen,'
Use all the observance of civility,
Like one well studied in a sad ostent
To please his grandam, never trust me more.

BASSANIO
Well, we shall see your bearing.

GRATIANO
Nay, but I bar to-night: you shall not gauge me
By what we do to-night.

BASSANIO
No, that were pity:
I would entreat you rather to put on
Your boldest suit of mirth, for we have friends
That purpose merriment. But fare you well:
I have some business.

GRATIANO
And I must to Lorenzo and the rest:
But we will visit you at supper-time.

Exeunt

SCENE III. The Same. A Room in Shylock's House.

Enter JESSICA and LAUNCELOT

JESSICA
I am sorry thou wilt leave my father so:
Our house is hell, and thou, a merry devil,
Didst rob it of some taste of tediousness.
But fare thee well, there is a ducat for thee:
And, Launcelot, soon at supper shalt thou see
Lorenzo, who is thy new master's guest:
Give him this letter; do it secretly;
And so farewell: I would not have my father
See me in talk with thee.

LAUNCELOT
Adieu! tears exhibit my tongue. Most beautiful
pagan, most sweet Jew! if a Christian did not play
the knave and get thee, I am much deceived. But,
adieu: these foolish drops do something drown my
manly spirit: adieu.

JESSICA
Farewell, good Launcelot.

Exit LAUNCELOT

Alack, what heinous sin is it in me
To be ashamed to be my father's child!
But though I am a daughter to his blood,
I am not to his manners. O Lorenzo,
If thou keep promise, I shall end this strife,
Become a Christian and thy loving wife.

Exit

SCENE IV. The Same. A Street.

Enter GRATIANO, LORENZO, SALARINO, and SALANIO

LORENZO
Nay, we will slink away in supper-time,
Disguise us at my lodging and return,
All in an hour.

GRATIANO
We have not made good preparation.

SALARINO
We have not spoke us yet of torchbearers.

SALANIO
'Tis vile, unless it may be quaintly order'd,
And better in my mind not undertook.

LORENZO
'Tis now but four o'clock: we have two hours
To furnish us.

Enter LAUNCELOT, with a letter

Friend Launcelot, what's the news?

LAUNCELOT
An it shall please you to break up
this, it shall seem to signify.

LORENZO
I know the hand: in faith, 'tis a fair hand;
And whiter than the paper it writ on
Is the fair hand that writ.

GRATIANO
Love-news, in faith.

LAUNCELOT

By your leave, sir.

LORENZO
Whither goest thou?

LAUNCELOT
Marry, sir, to bid my old master the
Jew to sup to-night with my new master the Christian.

LORENZO
Hold here, take this: tell gentle Jessica
I will not fail her; speak it privately.
Go, gentlemen,

Exit LAUNCELOT

Will you prepare you for this masque tonight?
I am provided of a torch-bearer.

SALANIO
Ay, marry, I'll be gone about it straight.

SALANIO
And so will I.

LORENZO
Meet me and Gratiano
At Gratiano's lodging some hour hence.

SALARINO
'Tis good we do so.

Exeunt SALARINO and SALANIO

GRATIANO
Was not that letter from fair Jessica?

LORENZO
I must needs tell thee all. She hath directed
How I shall take her from her father's house,
What gold and jewels she is furnish'd with,
What page's suit she hath in readiness.
If e'er the Jew her father come to heaven,
It will be for his gentle daughter's sake:
And never dare misfortune cross her foot,
Unless she do it under this excuse,
That she is issue to a faithless Jew.
Come, go with me; peruse this as thou goest:
Fair Jessica shall be my torch-beare r.

Exeunt

SCENE V. The Same. Before Shylock's House.

Enter SHYLOCK and LAUNCELOT

SHYLOCK
Well, thou shalt see, thy eyes shall be thy judge,
The difference of old Shylock and Bassanio:—
What, Jessica!—thou shalt not gormandise,
As thou hast done with me:—What, Jessica!—
And sleep and snore, and rend apparel out;—
Why, Jessica, I say!

LAUNCELOT
Why, Jessica!

SHYLOCK
Who bids thee call? I do not bid thee call.

LAUNCELOT
Your worship was wont to tell me that
I could do nothing without bidding.

Enter JESSICA

JESSICA
Call you? what is your will?

SHYLOCK
I am bid forth to supper, Jessica:
There are my keys. But wherefore should I go?
I am not bid for love; they flatter me:
But yet I'll go in hate, to feed upon
The prodigal Christian. Jessica, my girl,
Look to my house. I am right loath to go:
There is some ill a-brewing towards my rest,
For I did dream of money-bags to-night.

LAUNCELOT
I beseech you, sir, go: my young master doth expect your reproach.

SHYLOCK
So do I his.

LAUNCELOT
An they have conspired together, I will not say you shall see a masque; but if you do, then it was not for nothing that my nose fell a-bleeding on Black-Monday last at six o'clock i' the morning, falling out that year on Ash-Wednesday was four year, in the afternoon.

SHYLOCK
What, are there masques? Hear you me, Jessica:
Lock up my doors; and when you hear the drum
And the vile squealing of the wry-neck'd fife,
Clamber not you up to the casements then,
Nor thrust your head into the public street
To gaze on Christian fools with varnish'd faces,
But stop my house's ears, I mean my casements:
Let not the sound of shallow foppery enter
My sober house. By Jacob's staff, I swear,
I have no mind of feasting forth to-night:
But I will go. Go you before me, sirrah;
Say I will come.

LAUNCELOT
I will go before, sir. Mistress, look out at window, for all this, There will come a Christian boy, will be worth a Jewess' eye.

Exit

SHYLOCK
What says that fool of Hagar's offspring, ha?

JESSICA
His words were 'Farewell mistress;' nothing else.

SHYLOCK
The patch is kind enough, but a huge feeder;
Snail-slow in profit, and he sleeps by day
More than the wild-cat: drones hive not with me;
Therefore I part with him, and part with him
To one that would have him help to waste
His borrow'd purse. Well, Jessica, go in;
Perhaps I will return immediately:
Do as I bid you; shut doors after you:
Fast bind, fast find;
A proverb never stale in thrifty mind.

Exit

JESSICA
Farewell; and if my fortune be not crost,
I have a father, you a daughter, lost.

Exit

SCENE VI. The Same.

Enter GRATIANO and SALARINO, masqued

GRATIANO
This is the pent-house under which Lorenzo
Desired us to make stand.

SALARINO
His hour is almost past.

GRATIANO
And it is marvel he out-dwells his hour,
For lovers ever run before the clock.

SALARINO
O, ten times faster Venus' pigeons fly
To seal love's bonds new-made, than they are wont
To keep obliged faith unforfeited!

GRATIANO
That ever holds: who riseth from a feast
With that keen appetite that he sits down?
Where is the horse that doth untread again
His tedious measures with the unbated fire
That he did pace them first? All things that are,
Are with more spirit chased than enjoy'd.
How like a younker or a prodigal
The scarfed bark puts from her native bay,
Hugg'd and embraced by the strumpet wind!
How like the prodigal doth she return,
With over-weather'd ribs and ragged sails,
Lean, rent and beggar'd by the strumpet wind!

SALARINO
Here comes Lorenzo: more of this hereafter.

Enter LORENZO

LORENZO
Sweet friends, your patience for my long abode;
Not I, but my affairs, have made you wait:
When you shall please to play the thieves for wives,
I'll watch as long for you then. Approach;
Here dwells my father Jew. Ho! who's within?

Enter JESSICA, above, in boy's clothes

JESSICA
Who are you? Tell me, for more certainty,
Albeit I'll swear that I do know your tongue.

LORENZO
Lorenzo, and thy love.

JESSICA
Lorenzo, certain, and my love indeed,
For who love I so much? And now who knows
But you, Lorenzo, whether I am yours?

LORENZO
Heaven and thy thoughts are witness that thou art.

JESSICA
Here, catch this casket; it is worth the pains.
I am glad 'tis night, you do not look on me,
For I am much ashamed of my exchange:
But love is blind and lovers cannot see
The pretty follies that themselves commit;
For if they could, Cupid himself would blush
To see me thus transformed to a boy.

LORENZO
Descend, for you must be my torchbearer.

JESSICA
What, must I hold a candle to my shames?
They in themselves, good-sooth, are too too light.
Why, 'tis an office of discovery, love;
And I should be obscured.

LORENZO
So are you, sweet,
Even in the lovely garnish of a boy.
But come at once;
For the close night doth play the runaway,
And we are stay'd for at Bassanio's feast.

JESSICA
I will make fast the doors, and gild myself
With some more ducats, and be with you straight.

Exit above

GRATIANO
Now, by my hood, a Gentile and no Jew.

LORENZO
Beshrew me but I love her heartily;
For she is wise, if I can judge of her,
And fair she is, if that mine eyes be true,
And true she is, as she hath proved herself,
And therefore, like herself, wise, fair and true,
Shall she be placed in my constant soul.

Enter JESSICA, below

What, art thou come? On, gentlemen; away!
Our masquing mates by this time for us stay.

Exit with JESSICA and SALARINO.

Enter ANTONIO

ANTONIO
Who's there?

GRATIANO
Signior Antonio!

ANTONIO
Fie, fie, Gratiano! where are all the rest?
'Tis nine o'clock: our friends all stay for you.
No masque to-night: the wind is come about;
Bassanio presently will go aboard:
I have sent twenty out to seek for you.

GRATIANO
I am glad on't: I desire no more delight
Than to be under sail and gone to-night.

Exeunt

SCENE VII. Belmont. A Room in Portia's House.

Flourish of cornets. Enter PORTIA, with the PRINCE OF MOROCCO, and their trains

PORTIA
Go draw aside the curtains and discover
The several caskets to this noble prince.
Now make your choice.

MOROCCO
The first, of gold, who this inscription bears,
'Who chooseth me shall gain what many men desire;'
The second, silver, which this promise carries,
'Who chooseth me shall get as much as he deserves;'
This third, dull lead, with warning all as blunt,
'Who chooseth me must give and hazard all he hath.'
How shall I know if I do choose the right?

PORTIA
The one of them contains my picture, prince:
If you choose that, then I am yours withal.

MOROCCO

Some god direct my judgment! Let me see;
I will survey the inscriptions back again.
What says this leaden casket?
'Who chooseth me must give and hazard all he hath.'
Must give: for what? for lead? hazard for lead?
This casket threatens. Men that hazard all
Do it in hope of fair advantages:
A golden mind stoops not to shows of dross;
I'll then nor give nor hazard aught for lead.
What says the silver with her virgin hue?
'Who chooseth me shall get as much as he deserves.'
As much as he deserves! Pause there, Morocco,
And weigh thy value with an even hand:
If thou be'st rated by thy estimation,
Thou dost deserve enough; and yet enough
May not extend so far as to the lady:
And yet to be afeard of my deserving
Were but a weak disabling of myself.
As much as I deserve! Why, that's the lady:
I do in birth deserve her, and in fortunes,
In graces and in qualities of breeding;
But more than these, in love I do deserve.
What if I stray'd no further, but chose here?
Let's see once more this saying graved in gold
'Who chooseth me shall gain what many men desire.'
Why, that's the lady; all the world desires her;
From the four corners of the earth they come,
To kiss this shrine, this mortal-breathing saint:
The Hyrcanian deserts and the vasty wilds
Of wide Arabia are as thoroughfares now
For princes to come view fair Portia:
The watery kingdom, whose ambitious head
Spits in the face of heaven, is no bar
To stop the foreign spirits, but they come,
As o'er a brook, to see fair Portia.
One of these three contains her heavenly picture.
Is't like that lead contains her? 'Twere damnation
To think so base a thought: it were too gross
To rib her cerecloth in the obscure grave.
Or shall I think in silver she's immured,
Being ten times undervalued to tried gold?
O sinful thought! Never so rich a gem
Was set in worse than gold. They have in England
A coin that bears the figure of an angel
Stamped in gold, but that's insculp'd upon;
But here an angel in a golden bed
Lies all within. Deliver me the key:
Here do I choose, and thrive I as I may!

PORTIA
There, take it, prince; and if my form lie there,
Then I am yours.

He unlocks the golden casket

MOROCCO
O hell! what have we here?
A carrion Death, within whose empty eye
There is a written scroll! I'll read the writing.

Reads

All that glitters is not gold;
Often have you heard that told:
Many a man his life hath sold
But my outside to behold:
Gilded tombs do worms enfold.
Had you been as wise as bold,
Young in limbs, in judgment old,
Your answer had not been inscroll'd:
Fare you well; your suit is cold.
Cold, indeed; and labour lost:
Then, farewell, heat, and welcome, frost!
Portia, adieu. I have too grieved a heart
To take a tedious leave: thus losers part.

Exit with his train.

Flourish of cornets

PORTIA
A gentle riddance. Draw the curtains, go.
Let all of his complexion choose me so.

Exeunt

SCENE VIII. Venice. A Street.

Enter SALARINO and SALANIO

SALARINO
Why, man, I saw Bassanio under sail:
With him is Gratiano gone along;
And in their ship I am sure Lorenzo is not.

SALANIO
The villain Jew with outcries raised the duke,
Who went with him to search Bassanio's ship.

SALARINO

He came too late, the ship was under sail:
But there the duke was given to understand
That in a gondola were seen together
Lorenzo and his amorous Jessica:
Besides, Antonio certified the duke
They were not with Bassanio in his ship.

SALANIO

I never heard a passion so confused,
So strange, outrageous, and so variable,
As the dog Jew did utter in the streets:
'My daughter! O my ducats! O my daughter!
Fled with a Christian! O my Christian ducats!
Justice! the law! my ducats, and my daughter!
A sealed bag, two sealed bags of ducats,
Of double ducats, stolen from me by my daughter!
And jewels, two stones, two rich and precious stones,
Stolen by my daughter! Justice! find the girl;
She hath the stones upon her, and the ducats.'

SALARINO

Why, all the boys in Venice follow him,
Crying, his stones, his daughter, and his ducats.

SALANIO

Let good Antonio look he keep his day,
Or he shall pay for this.

SALARINO

Marry, well remember'd.
I reason'd with a Frenchman yesterday,
Who told me, in the narrow seas that part
The French and English, there miscarried
A vessel of our country richly fraught:
I thought upon Antonio when he told me;
And wish'd in silence that it were not his.

SALANIO

You were best to tell Antonio what you hear;
Yet do not suddenly, for it may grieve him.

SALARINO

A kinder gentleman treads not the earth.
I saw Bassanio and Antonio part:
Bassanio told him he would make some speed
Of his return: he answer'd, 'Do not so;
Slubber not business for my sake, Bassanio
But stay the very riping of the time;
And for the Jew's bond which he hath of me,

Let it not enter in your mind of love:
Be merry, and employ your chiefest thoughts
To courtship and such fair ostents of love
As shall conveniently become you there:'
And even there, his eye being big with tears,
Turning his face, he put his hand behind him,
And with affection wondrous sensible
He wrung Bassanio's hand; and so they parted.

SALANIO
I think he only loves the world for him.
I pray thee, let us go and find him out
And quicken his embraced heaviness
With some delight or other.

SALARINO
Do we so.

Exeunt

SCENE IX. Belmont. A Room in Portia's House.

Enter NERISSA with a Servitor

NERISSA
Quick, quick, I pray thee; draw the curtain straight:
The Prince of Arragon hath ta'en his oath,
And comes to his election presently.

Flourish of cornets.

Enter the PRINCE OF ARRAGON, PORTIA, and their trains

PORTIA
Behold, there stand the caskets, noble prince:
If you choose that wherein I am contain'd,
Straight shall our nuptial rites be solemnized:
But if you fail, without more speech, my lord,
You must be gone from hence immediately.

ARRAGON
I am enjoin'd by oath to observe three things:
First, never to unfold to any one
Which casket 'twas I chose; next, if I fail
Of the right casket, never in my life
To woo a maid in way of marriage: Lastly,
If I do fail in fortune of my choice,
Immediately to leave you and be gone.

PORTIA
To these injunctions every one doth swear
That comes to hazard for my worthless self.

ARRAGON
And so have I address'd me. Fortune now
To my heart's hope! Gold; silver; and base lead.
'Who chooseth me must give and hazard all he hath.'
You shall look fairer, ere I give or hazard.
What says the golden chest? ha! let me see:
'Who chooseth me shall gain what many men desire.'
What many men desire! that 'many' may be meant
By the fool multitude, that choose by show,
Not learning more than the fond eye doth teach;
Which pries not to the interior, but, like the martlet,
Builds in the weather on the outward wall,
Even in the force and road of casualty.
I will not choose what many men desire,
Because I will not jump with common spirits
And rank me with the barbarous multitudes.
Why, then to thee, thou silver treasure-house;
Tell me once more what title thou dost bear:
'Who chooseth me shall get as much as he deserves:'
And well said too; for who shall go about
To cozen fortune and be honourable
Without the stamp of merit? Let none presume
To wear an undeserved dignity.
O, that estates, degrees and offices
Were not derived corruptly, and that clear honour
Were purchased by the merit of the wearer!
How many then should cover that stand bare!
How many be commanded that command!
How much low peasantry would then be glean'd
From the true seed of honour! and how much honour
Pick'd from the chaff and ruin of the times
To be new-varnish'd! Well, but to my choice:
'Who chooseth me shall get as much as he deserves.'
I will assume desert. Give me a key for this,
And instantly unlock my fortunes here.

He opens the silver casket

PORTIA
Too long a pause for that which you find there.

ARRAGON
What's here? the portrait of a blinking idiot,
Presenting me a schedule! I will read it.
How much unlike art thou to Portia!
How much unlike my hopes and my deservings!
'Who chooseth me shall have as much as he deserves.'

Did I deserve no more than a fool's head?
Is that my prize? are my deserts no better?

PORTIA
To offend, and judge, are distinct offices
And of opposed natures.

ARRAGON
What is here?

Reads

The fire seven times tried this:
Seven times tried that judgment is,
That did never choose amiss.
Some there be that shadows kiss;
Such have but a shadow's bliss:
There be fools alive, I wis,
Silver'd o'er; and so was this.
Take what wife you will to bed,
I will ever be your head:
So be gone: you are sped.
Still more fool I shall appear
By the time I linger here
With one fool's head I came to woo,
But I go away with two.
Sweet, adieu. I'll keep my oath,
Patiently to bear my wroth.

Exeunt ARRAGAN and train

PORTIA
Thus hath the candle singed the moth.
O, these deliberate fools! when they do choose,
They have the wisdom by their wit to lose.

NERISSA
The ancient saying is no heresy,
Hanging and wiving goes by destiny.

PORTIA
Come, draw the curtain, Nerissa.

Enter a SERVANT

SERVANT
Where is my lady?

PORTIA
Here: what would my lord?

SERVANT
Madam, there is alighted at your gate
A young Venetian, one that comes before
To signify the approaching of his lord;
From whom he bringeth sensible regreets,
To wit, besides commends and courteous breath,
Gifts of rich value. Yet I have not seen
So likely an ambassador of love:
A day in April never came so sweet,
To show how costly summer was at hand,
As this fore-spurrer comes before his lord.

PORTIA
No more, I pray thee: I am half afeard
Thou wilt say anon he is some kin to thee,
Thou spend'st such high-day wit in praising him.
Come, come, Nerissa; for I long to see
Quick Cupid's post that comes so mannerly.

NERISSA
Bassanio, lord Love, if thy will it be!

Exeunt

ACT III

SCENE I. Venice. A Street.

Enter SALANIO and SALARINO

SALANIO
Now, what news on the Rialto?

SALARINO
Why, yet it lives there uncheck'd that Antonio hath a ship of rich lading wrecked on the narrow seas;
the Goodwins, I think they call the place; a very dangerous flat and fatal, where the carcasses of
many a tall ship lie buried, as they say, if my gossip Report be an honest woman of her word.

SALANIO
I would she were as lying a gossip in that as ever knapped ginger or made her neighbours believe she
wept for the death of a third husband. But it is true, without any slips of prolixity or crossing the
plain highway of talk, that the good Antonio, the honest Antonio, O that I had a title good enough to
keep his name company!

SALARINO
Come, the full stop.

SALANIO
Ha! what sayest thou? Why, the end is, he hath lost a ship.

SALARINO

I would it might prove the end of his losses.

SALANIO

Let me say 'amen' betimes, lest the devil cross my prayer, for here he comes in the likeness of a Jew.

Enter SHYLOCK

How now, Shylock! what news among the merchants?

SHYLOCK

You know, none so well, none so well as you, of my daughter's flight.

SALARINO

That's certain: I, for my part, knew the tailor that made the wings she flew withal.

SALANIO

And Shylock, for his own part, knew the bird was fledged; and then it is the complexion of them all to leave the dam.

SHYLOCK

She is damned for it.

SALANIO

That's certain, if the devil may be her judge.

SHYLOCK

My own flesh and blood to rebel!

SALANIO

Out upon it, old carrion! rebels it at these years?

SHYLOCK

I say, my daughter is my flesh and blood.

SALARINO

There is more difference between thy flesh and hers than between jet and ivory; more between your bloods than there is between red wine and rhenish. But tell us, do you hear whether Antonio have had any loss at sea or no?

SHYLOCK

There I have another bad match: a bankrupt, a prodigal, who dare scarce show his head on the Rialto; a beggar, that was used to come so smug upon the mart; let him look to his bond: he was wont to call me usurer; let him look to his bond: he was wont to lend money for a Christian courtesy; let him look to his bond.

SALARINO

Why, I am sure, if he forfeit, thou wilt not take his flesh: what's that good for?

SHYLOCK

To bait fish withal: if it will feed nothing else, it will feed my revenge. He hath disgraced me, and hindered me half a million; laughed at my losses, mocked at my gains, scorned my nation, thwarted my bargains, cooled my friends, heated mine enemies; and what's his reason? I am a Jew. Hath not a Jew eyes? hath not a Jew hands, organs, dimensions, senses, affections, passions? fed with the same food, hurt with the same weapons, subject to the same diseases, healed by the same means, warmed and cooled by the same winter and summer, as a Christian is? If you prick us, do we not bleed? if you tickle us, do we not laugh? if you poison us, do we not die? and if you wrong us, shall we not revenge? If we are like you in the rest, we will resemble you in that. If a Jew wrong a Christian, what is his humility? Revenge. If a Christian wrong a Jew, what should his sufferance be by Christian example? Why, revenge. The villany you teach me, I will execute, and it shall go hard but I will better the instruction.

Enter a SERVANT

SERVANT
Gentlemen, my master Antonio is at his house and desires to speak with you both.

SALARINO
We have been up and down to seek him.

Enter TUBAL

SALANIO
Here comes another of the tribe: a third cannot be matched, unless the devil himself turn Jew.

Exeunt SALANIO, SALARINO, and SERVANT

SHYLOCK
How now, Tubal! what news from Genoa? hast thou found my daughter?

TUBAL
I often came where I did hear of her, but cannot find her.

SHYLOCK
Why, there, there, there, there! a diamond gone, cost me two thousand ducats in Frankfort! The curse never fell upon our nation till now; I never felt it till now: two thousand ducats in that; and other precious, precious jewels. I would my daughter were dead at my foot, and the jewels in her ear! would she were hearsed at my foot, and the ducats in her coffin! No news of them? Why, so: and I know not what's spent in the search: why, thou loss upon loss! the thief gone with so much, and so much to find the thief; and no satisfaction, no revenge: nor no in luck stirring but what lights on my shoulders; no sighs but of my breathing; no tears but of my shedding.

TUBAL
Yes, other men have ill luck too: Antonio, as I heard in Genoa,—

SHYLOCK
What, what, what? ill luck, ill luck?

TUBAL
Hath an argosy cast away, coming from Tripolis.

SHYLOCK
I thank God, I thank God. Is't true, is't true?

TUBAL
I spoke with some of the sailors that escaped the wreck.

SHYLOCK
I thank thee, good Tubal: good news, good news!
Ha, ha! where? in Genoa?

TUBAL
Your daughter spent in Genoa, as I heard, in one night fourscore ducats.

SHYLOCK
Thou stickest a dagger in me: I shall never see my gold again: fourscore ducats at a sitting!
fourscore ducats!

TUBAL
There came divers of Antonio's creditors in my company to Venice, that swear he cannot choose but
break.

SHYLOCK
I am very glad of it: I'll plague him; I'll torture him: I am glad of it.

TUBAL
One of them showed me a ring that he had of your daughter for a monkey.

SHYLOCK
Out upon her! Thou torturest me, Tubal: it was my turquoise; I had it of Leah when I was a bachelor:
I would not have given it for a wilderness of monkeys.

TUBAL
But Antonio is certainly undone.

SHYLOCK
Nay, that's true, that's very true. Go, Tubal, fee me an officer; bespeak him a fortnight before. I
will have the heart of him, if he forfeit; for, were he out of Venice, I can make what merchandise I
will. Go, go, Tubal, and meet me at our synagogue; go, good Tubal; at our synagogue, Tubal.

Exeunt

SCENE II. Belmont. A Room in Portia's House.

Enter BASSANIO, PORTIA, GRATIANO, NERISSA, and Attendants

PORTIA
I pray you, tarry: pause a day or two
Before you hazard; for, in choosing wrong,
I lose your company: therefore forbear awhile.

There's something tells me, but it is not love,
I would not lose you; and you know yourself,
Hate counsels not in such a quality.
But lest you should not understand me well,—
And yet a maiden hath no tongue but thought,—
I would detain you here some month or two
Before you venture for me. I could teach you
How to choose right, but I am then forsworn;
So will I never be: so may you miss me;
But if you do, you'll make me wish a sin,
That I had been forsworn. Beshrew your eyes,
They have o'erlook'd me and divided me;
One half of me is yours, the other half yours,
Mine own, I would say; but if mine, then yours,
And so all yours. O, these naughty times
Put bars between the owners and their rights!
And so, though yours, not yours. Prove it so,
Let fortune go to hell for it, not I.
I speak too long; but 'tis to peize the time,
To eke it and to draw it out in length,
To stay you from election.

BASSANIO
Let me choose
For as I am, I live upon the rack.

PORTIA
Upon the rack, Bassanio! then confess
What treason there is mingled with your love.

BASSANIO
None but that ugly treason of mistrust,
Which makes me fear the enjoying of my love:
There may as well be amity and life
'Tween snow and fire, as treason and my love.

PORTIA
Ay, but I fear you speak upon the rack,
Where men enforced do speak anything.

BASSANIO
Promise me life, and I'll confess the truth.

PORTIA
Well then, confess and live.

BASSANIO
'Confess' and 'love'
Had been the very sum of my confession:
O happy torment, when my torturer

Doth teach me answers for deliverance!
But let me to my fortune and the caskets.

PORTIA
Away, then! I am lock'd in one of them:
If you do love me, you will find me out.
Nerissa and the rest, stand all aloof.
Let music sound while he doth make his choice;
Then, if he lose, he makes a swan-like end,
Fading in music: that the comparison
May stand more proper, my eye shall be the stream
And watery death-bed for him. He may win;
And what is music then? Then music is
Even as the flourish when true subjects bow
To a new-crowned monarch: such it is
As are those dulcet sounds in break of day
That creep into the dreaming bridegroom's ear,
And summon him to marriage. Now he goes,
With no less presence, but with much more love,
Than young Alcides, when he did redeem
The virgin tribute paid by howling Troy
To the sea-monster: I stand for sacrifice
The rest aloof are the Dardanian wives,
With bleared visages, come forth to view
The issue of the exploit. Go, Hercules!
Live thou, I live: with much, much more dismay
I view the fight than thou that makest the fray.

Music, whilst BASSANIO comments on the caskets to himself

SONG.
Tell me where is fancy bred,
Or in the heart, or in the head?
How begot, how nourished?
Reply, reply.
It is engender'd in the eyes,
With gazing fed; and fancy dies
In the cradle where it lies.
Let us all ring fancy's knell
I'll begin it, Ding, dong, bell.

ALL
Ding, dong, bell.

BASSANIO
So may the outward shows be least themselves:
The world is still deceived with ornament.
In law, what plea so tainted and corrupt,
But, being seasoned with a gracious voice,
Obscures the show of evil? In religion,
What damned error, but some sober brow

Will bless it and approve it with a text,
Hiding the grossness with fair ornament?
There is no vice so simple but assumes
Some mark of virtue on his outward parts:
How many cowards, whose hearts are all as false
As stairs of sand, wear yet upon their chins
The beards of Hercules and frowning Mars;
Who, inward search'd, have livers white as milk;
And these assume but valour's excrement
To render them redoubted! Look on beauty,
And you shall see 'tis purchased by the weight;
Which therein works a miracle in nature,
Making them lightest that wear most of it:
So are those crisped snaky golden locks
Which make such wanton gambols with the wind,
Upon supposed fairness, often known
To be the dowry of a second head,
The skull that bred them in the sepulchre.
Thus ornament is but the guiled shore
To a most dangerous sea; the beauteous scarf
Veiling an Indian beauty; in a word,
The seeming truth which cunning times put on
To entrap the wisest. Therefore, thou gaudy gold,
Hard food for Midas, I will none of thee;
Nor none of thee, thou pale and common drudge
'Tween man and man: but thou, thou meagre lead,
Which rather threatenest than dost promise aught,
Thy paleness moves me more than eloquence;
And here choose I; joy be the consequence!

PORTIA
[Aside] How all the other passions fleet to air,
As doubtful thoughts, and rash-embraced despair,
And shuddering fear, and green-eyed jealousy! O love,
Be moderate; allay thy ecstasy,
In measure rein thy joy; scant this excess.
I feel too much thy blessing: make it less,
For fear I surfeit.

BASSANIO
What find I here?

Opening the leaden casket

Fair Portia's counterfeit! What demi-god
Hath come so near creation? Move these eyes?
Or whether, riding on the balls of mine,
Seem they in motion? Here are sever'd lips,
Parted with sugar breath: so sweet a bar
Should sunder such sweet friends. Here in her hairs
The painter plays the spider and hath woven

A golden mesh to entrap the hearts of men,
Faster than gnats in cobwebs; but her eyes,—
How could he see to do them? having made one,
Methinks it should have power to steal both his
And leave itself unfurnish'd. Yet look, how far
The substance of my praise doth wrong this shadow
In underprizing it, so far this shadow
Doth limp behind the substance. Here's the scroll,
The continent and summary of my fortune.

Reads

You that choose not by the view,
Chance as fair and choose as true!
Since this fortune falls to you,
Be content and seek no new,
If you be well pleased with this
And hold your fortune for your bliss,
Turn you where your lady is
And claim her with a loving kiss.
A gentle scroll. Fair lady, by your leave;
I come by note, to give and to receive.
Like one of two contending in a prize,
That thinks he hath done well in people's eyes,
Hearing applause and universal shout,
Giddy in spirit, still gazing in a doubt
Whether these pearls of praise be his or no;
So, thrice fair lady, stand I, even so;
As doubtful whether what I see be true,
Until confirm'd, sign'd, ratified by you.

PORTIA
You see me, Lord Bassanio, where I stand,
Such as I am: though for myself alone
I would not be ambitious in my wish,
To wish myself much better; yet, for you
I would be trebled twenty times myself;
A thousand times more fair, ten thousand times more rich;
That only to stand high in your account,
I might in virtue, beauties, livings, friends,
Exceed account; but the full sum of me
Is sum of something, which, to term in gross,
Is an unlesson'd girl, unschool'd, unpractised;
Happy in this, she is not yet so old
But she may learn; happier than this,
She is not bred so dull but she can learn;
Happiest of all is that her gentle spirit
Commits itself to yours to be directed,
As from her lord, her governor, her king.
Myself and what is mine to you and yours
Is now converted: but now I was the lord

Of this fair mansion, master of my servants,
Queen o'er myself: and even now, but now,
This house, these servants and this same myself
Are yours, my lord: I give them with this ring;
Which when you part from, lose, or give away,
Let it presage the ruin of your love
And be my vantage to exclaim on you.

BASSANIO
Madam, you have bereft me of all words,
Only my blood speaks to you in my veins;
And there is such confusion in my powers,
As after some oration fairly spoke
By a beloved prince, there doth appear
Among the buzzing pleased multitude;
Where every something, being blent together,
Turns to a wild of nothing, save of joy,
Express'd and not express'd. But when this ring
Parts from this finger, then parts life from hence:
O, then be bold to say Bassanio's dead!

NERISSA
My lord and lady, it is now our time,
That have stood by and seen our wishes prosper,
To cry, good joy: good joy, my lord and lady!

GRATIANO
My lord Bassanio and my gentle lady,
I wish you all the joy that you can wish;
For I am sure you can wish none from me:
And when your honours mean to solemnize
The bargain of your faith, I do beseech you,
Even at that time I may be married too.

BASSANIO
With all my heart, so thou canst get a wife.

GRATIANO
I thank your lordship, you have got me one.
My eyes, my lord, can look as swift as yours:
You saw the mistress, I beheld the maid;
You loved, I loved for intermission.
No more pertains to me, my lord, than you.
Your fortune stood upon the casket there,
And so did mine too, as the matter falls;
For wooing here until I sweat again,
And sweating until my very roof was dry
With oaths of love, at last, if promise last,
I got a promise of this fair one here
To have her love, provided that your fortune
Achieved her mistress.

PORTIA
Is this true, Nerissa?

NERISSA
Madam, it is, so you stand pleased withal.

BASSANIO
And do you, Gratiano, mean good faith?

GRATIANO
Yes, faith, my lord.

BASSANIO
Our feast shall be much honour'd in your marriage.

GRATIANO
We'll play with them the first boy for a thousand ducats.

NERISSA
What, and stake down?

GRATIANO
No; we shall ne'er win at that sport, and stake down.
But who comes here? Lorenzo and his infidel?
What, and my old Venetian friend Salerio?

Enter LORENZO, JESSICA, and SALERIO, a Messenger from Venice

BASSANIO
Lorenzo and Salerio, welcome hither;
If that the youth of my new interest here
Have power to bid you welcome. By your leave,
I bid my very friends and countrymen,
Sweet Portia, welcome.

PORTIA
So do I, my lord:
They are entirely welcome.

LORENZO
I thank your honour. For my part, my lord,
My purpose was not to have seen you here;
But meeting with Salerio by the way,
He did entreat me, past all saying nay,
To come with him along.

SALERIO
I did, my lord;
And I have reason for it. Signior Antonio
Commends him to you.

Gives BASSANIO a letter

BASSANIO
Ere I ope his letter,
I pray you, tell me how my good friend doth.

SALERIO
Not sick, my lord, unless it be in mind;
Nor well, unless in mind: his letter there
Will show you his estate.

GRATIANO
Nerissa, cheer yon stranger; bid her welcome.
Your hand, Salerio: what's the news from Venice?
How doth that royal merchant, good Antonio?
I know he will be glad of our success;
We are the Jasons, we have won the fleece.

SALERIO
I would you had won the fleece that he hath lost.

PORTIA
There are some shrewd contents in yon same paper,
That steals the colour from Bassanio's cheek:
Some dear friend dead; else nothing in the world
Could turn so much the constitution
Of any constant man. What, worse and worse!
With leave, Bassanio: I am half yourself,
And I must freely have the half of anything
That this same paper brings you.

BASSANIO
O sweet Portia,
Here are a few of the unpleasant'st words
That ever blotted paper! Gentle lady,
When I did first impart my love to you,
I freely told you, all the wealth I had
Ran in my veins, I was a gentleman;
And then I told you true: and yet, dear lady,
Rating myself at nothing, you shall see
How much I was a braggart. When I told you
My state was nothing, I should then have told you
That I was worse than nothing; for, indeed,
I have engaged myself to a dear friend,
Engaged my friend to his mere enemy,
To feed my means. Here is a letter, lady;
The paper as the body of my friend,
And every word in it a gaping wound,
Issuing life-blood. But is it true, Salerio?
Have all his ventures fail'd? What, not one hit?

From Tripolis, from Mexico and England,
From Lisbon, Barbary and India?
And not one vessel 'scape the dreadful touch
Of merchant-marring rocks?

SALERIO
Not one, my lord.
Besides, it should appear, that if he had
The present money to discharge the Jew,
He would not take it. Never did I know
A creature, that did bear the shape of man,
So keen and greedy to confound a man:
He plies the duke at morning and at night,
And doth impeach the freedom of the state,
If they deny him justice: twenty merchants,
The duke himself, and the magnificoes
Of greatest port, have all persuaded with him;
But none can drive him from the envious plea
Of forfeiture, of justice and his bond.

JESSICA
When I was with him I have heard him swear
To Tubal and to Chus, his countrymen,
That he would rather have Antonio's flesh
Than twenty times the value of the sum
That he did owe him: and I know, my lord,
If law, authority and power deny not,
It will go hard with poor Antonio.

PORTIA
Is it your dear friend that is thus in trouble?

BASSANIO
The dearest friend to me, the kindest man,
The best-condition'd and unwearied spirit
In doing courtesies, and one in whom
The ancient Roman honour more appears
Than any that draws breath in Italy.

PORTIA
What sum owes he the Jew?

BASSANIO
For me three thousand ducats.

PORTIA
What, no more?
Pay him six thousand, and deface the bond;
Double six thousand, and then treble that,
Before a friend of this description
Shall lose a hair through Bassanio's fault.

First go with me to church and call me wife,
And then away to Venice to your friend;
For never shall you lie by Portia's side
With an unquiet soul. You shall have gold
To pay the petty debt twenty times over:
When it is paid, bring your true friend along.
My maid Nerissa and myself meantime
Will live as maids and widows. Come, away!
For you shall hence upon your wedding-day:
Bid your friends welcome, show a merry cheer:
Since you are dear bought, I will love you dear.
But let me hear the letter of your friend.

BASSANIO
[Reads] Sweet Bassanio, my ships have all
miscarried, my creditors grow cruel, my estate is
very low, my bond to the Jew is forfeit; and since
in paying it, it is impossible I should live, all
debts are cleared between you and I, if I might but
see you at my death. Notwithstanding, use your
pleasure: if your love do not persuade you to come,
let not my letter.

PORTIA
O love, dispatch all business, and be gone!

BASSANIO
Since I have your good leave to go away,
I will make haste: but, till I come again,
No bed shall e'er be guilty of my stay,
No rest be interposer 'twixt us twain.

Exeunt

SCENE III. Venice. A Street.

Enter SHYLOCK, SALARINO, ANTONIO, and Gaoler

SHYLOCK
Gaoler, look to him: tell not me of mercy;
This is the fool that lent out money gratis:
Gaoler, look to him.

ANTONIO
Hear me yet, good Shylock.

SHYLOCK
I'll have my bond; speak not against my bond:
I have sworn an oath that I will have my bond.

Thou call'dst me dog before thou hadst a cause;
But, since I am a dog, beware my fangs:
The duke shall grant me justice. I do wonder,
Thou naughty gaoler, that thou art so fond
To come abroad with him at his request.

ANTONIO
I pray thee, hear me speak.

SHYLOCK
I'll have my bond; I will not hear thee speak:
I'll have my bond; and therefore speak no more.
I'll not be made a soft and dull-eyed fool,
To shake the head, relent, and sigh, and yield
To Christian intercessors. Follow not;
I'll have no speaking: I will have my bond.

Exit

SALARINO
It is the most impenetrable cur
That ever kept with men.

ANTONIO
Let him alone:
I'll follow him no more with bootless prayers.
He seeks my life; his reason well I know:
I oft deliver'd from his forfeitures
Many that have at times made moan to me;
Therefore he hates me.

SALARINO
I am sure the duke
Will never grant this forfeiture to hold.

ANTONIO
The duke cannot deny the course of law:
For the commodity that strangers have
With us in Venice, if it be denied,
Will much impeach the justice of his state;
Since that the trade and profit of the city
Consisteth of all nations. Therefore, go:
These griefs and losses have so bated me,
That I shall hardly spare a pound of flesh
To-morrow to my bloody creditor.
Well, gaoler, on. Pray God, Bassanio come
To see me pay his debt, and then I care not!

Exeunt

Enter PORTIA, NERISSA, LORENZO, JESSICA, and BALTHASAR

LORENZO
Madam, although I speak it in your presence,
You have a noble and a true conceit
Of godlike amity; which appears most strongly
In bearing thus the absence of your lord.
But if you knew to whom you show this honour,
How true a gentleman you send relief,
How dear a lover of my lord your husband,
I know you would be prouder of the work
Than customary bounty can enforce you.

PORTIA
I never did repent for doing good,
Nor shall not now: for in companions
That do converse and waste the time together,
Whose souls do bear an equal yoke Of love,
There must be needs a like proportion
Of lineaments, of manners and of spirit;
Which makes me think that this Antonio,
Being the bosom lover of my lord,
Must needs be like my lord. If it be so,
How little is the cost I have bestow'd
In purchasing the semblance of my soul
From out the state of hellish misery!
This comes too near the praising of myself;
Therefore no more of it: hear other things.
Lorenzo, I commit into your hands
The husbandry and manage of my house
Until my lord's return: for mine own part,
I have toward heaven breathed a secret vow
To live in prayer and contemplation,
Only attended by Nerissa here,
Until her husband and my lord's return:
There is a monastery two miles off;
And there will we abide. I do desire you
Not to deny this imposition;
The which my love and some necessity
Now lays upon you.

LORENZO
Madam, with all my heart;
I shall obey you in all fair commands.

PORTIA
My people do already know my mind,
And will acknowledge you and Jessica

In place of Lord Bassanio and myself.
And so farewell, till we shall meet again.

LORENZO
Fair thoughts and happy hours attend on you!

JESSICA
I wish your ladyship all heart's content.

PORTIA
I thank you for your wish, and am well pleased
To wish it back on you: fare you well Jessica.

Exeunt JESSICA and LORENZO

Now, Balthasar,
As I have ever found thee honest-true,
So let me find thee still. Take this same letter,
And use thou all the endeavour of a man
In speed to Padua: see thou render this
Into my cousin's hand, Doctor Bellario;
And, look, what notes and garments he doth give thee,
Bring them, I pray thee, with imagined speed
Unto the tranect, to the common ferry
Which trades to Venice. Waste no time in words,
But get thee gone: I shall be there before thee.

BALTHASAR
Madam, I go with all convenient speed.

Exit

PORTIA
Come on, Nerissa; I have work in hand
That you yet know not of: we'll see our husbands
Before they think of us.

NERISSA
Shall they see us?

PORTIA
They shall, Nerissa; but in such a habit,
That they shall think we are accomplished
With that we lack. I'll hold thee any wager,
When we are both accoutred like young men,
I'll prove the prettier fellow of the two,
And wear my dagger with the braver grace,
And speak between the change of man and boy
With a reed voice, and turn two mincing steps
Into a manly stride, and speak of frays
Like a fine bragging youth, and tell quaint lies,

How honourable ladies sought my love,
Which I denying, they fell sick and died;
I could not do withal; then I'll repent,
And wish for all that, that I had not killed them;
And twenty of these puny lies I'll tell,
That men shall swear I have discontinued school
Above a twelvemonth. I have within my mind
A thousand raw tricks of these bragging Jacks,
Which I will practise.

NERISSA
Why, shall we turn to men?

PORTIA
Fie, what a question's that,
If thou wert near a lewd interpreter!
But come, I'll tell thee all my whole device
When I am in my coach, which stays for us
At the park gate; and therefore haste away,
For we must measure twenty miles to-day.

Exeunt

SCENE V. The Same. A Garden.

Enter LAUNCELOT and JESSICA

LAUNCELOT
Yes, truly; for, look you, the sins of the father are to be laid upon the children: therefore, I promise
ye, I fear you. I was always plain with you, and so now I speak my agitation of the matter: therefore
be of good cheer, for truly I think you are damned. There is but one hope in it that can do you any
good; and that is but a kind of bastard hope neither.

JESSICA
And what hope is that, I pray thee?

LAUNCELOT
Marry, you may partly hope that your father got you not, that you are not the Jew's daughter.

JESSICA
That were a kind of bastard hope, indeed: so the sins of my mother should be visited upon me.

LAUNCELOT
Truly then I fear you are damned both by father and mother: thus when I shun Scylla, your father, I
fall into Charybdis, your mother: well, you are gone both ways.

JESSICA
I shall be saved by my husband; he hath made me a Christian.

LAUNCELOT
Truly, the more to blame he: we were Christians enow before; e'en as many as could well live, one by another. This making Christians will raise the price of hogs: if we grow all to be pork-eaters, we shall not shortly have a rasher on the coals for money.

Enter LORENZO

JESSICA
I'll tell my husband, Launcelot, what you say: here he comes.

LORENZO
I shall grow jealous of you shortly, Launcelot, if you thus get my wife into corners.

JESSICA
Nay, you need not fear us, Lorenzo: Launcelot and I are out. He tells me flatly, there is no mercy for me in heaven, because I am a Jew's daughter: and he says, you are no good member of the commonwealth, for in converting Jews to Christians, you raise the price of pork.

LORENZO
I shall answer that better to the commonwealth than you can the getting up of the negro's belly: the Moor is with child by you, Launcelot.

LAUNCELOT
It is much that the Moor should be more than reason: but if she be less than an honest woman, she is indeed more than I took her for.

LORENZO
How every fool can play upon the word! I think the best grace of wit will shortly turn into silence, and discourse grow commendable in none only but parrots. Go in, sirrah; bid them prepare for dinner.

LAUNCELOT
That is done, sir; they have all stomachs.

LORENZO
Goodly Lord, what a wit-snapper are you! then bid them prepare dinner.

LAUNCELOT
That is done too, sir; only 'cover' is the word.

LORENZO
Will you cover then, sir?

LAUNCELOT
Not so, sir, neither; I know my duty.

LORENZO
Yet more quarrelling with occasion! Wilt thou show the whole wealth of thy wit in an instant? I pray tree, understand a plain man in his plain meaning: go to thy fellows; bid them cover the table, serve in the meat, and we will come in to dinner.

LAUNCELOT
For the table, sir, it shall be served in; for the meat, sir, it shall be covered; for your coming in to dinner, sir, why, let it be as humours and conceits shall govern.

Exit

LORENZO
O dear discretion, how his words are suited!
The fool hath planted in his memory
An army of good words; and I do know
A many fools, that stand in better place,
Garnish'd like him, that for a tricksy word
Defy the matter. How cheerest thou, Jessica?
And now, good sweet, say thy opinion,
How dost thou like the Lord Bassanio's wife?

JESSICA
Past all expressing. It is very meet
The Lord Bassanio live an upright life;
For, having such a blessing in his lady,
He finds the joys of heaven here on earth;
And if on earth he do not mean it, then
In reason he should never come to heaven
Why, if two gods should play some heavenly match
And on the wager lay two earthly women,
And Portia one, there must be something else
Pawn'd with the other, for the poor rude world
Hath not her fellow.

LORENZO
Even such a husband
Hast thou of me as she is for a wife.

JESSICA
Nay, but ask my opinion too of that.

LORENZO
I will anon: first, let us go to dinner.

JESSICA
Nay, let me praise you while I have a stomach.

LORENZO
No, pray thee, let it serve for table-talk;
'Then, howso'er thou speak'st, 'mong other things
I shall digest it.

JESSICA
Well, I'll set you forth.

Exeunt

SCENE I. Venice. A Court of Justice.

Enter the DUKE, the Magnificoes, ANTONIO, BASSANIO, GRATIANO, SALERIO, and others

DUKE
What, is Antonio here?

ANTONIO
Ready, so please your grace.

DUKE
I am sorry for thee: thou art come to answer
A stony adversary, an inhuman wretch
Uncapable of pity, void and empty
From any dram of mercy.

ANTONIO
I have heard
Your grace hath ta'en great pains to qualify
His rigorous course; but since he stands obdurate
And that no lawful means can carry me
Out of his envy's reach, I do oppose
My patience to his fury, and am arm'd
To suffer, with a quietness of spirit,
The very tyranny and rage of his.

DUKE
Go one, and call the Jew into the court.

SALERIO
He is ready at the door: he comes, my lord.

Enter SHYLOCK

DUKE
Make room, and let him stand before our face.
Shylock, the world thinks, and I think so too,
That thou but lead'st this fashion of thy malice
To the last hour of act; and then 'tis thought
Thou'lt show thy mercy and remorse more strange
Than is thy strange apparent cruelty;
And where thou now exact'st the penalty,
Which is a pound of this poor merchant's flesh,
Thou wilt not only loose the forfeiture,
But, touch'd with human gentleness and love,
Forgive a moiety of the principal;

Glancing an eye of pity on his losses,
That have of late so huddled on his back,
Enow to press a royal merchant down
And pluck commiseration of his state
From brassy bosoms and rough hearts of flint,
From stubborn Turks and Tartars, never train'd
To offices of tender courtesy.
We all expect a gentle answer, Jew.

SHYLOCK
I have possess'd your grace of what I purpose;
And by our holy Sabbath have I sworn
To have the due and forfeit of my bond:
If you deny it, let the danger light
Upon your charter and your city's freedom.
You'll ask me, why I rather choose to have
A weight of carrion flesh than to receive
Three thousand ducats: I'll not answer that:
But, say, it is my humour: is it answer'd?
What if my house be troubled with a rat
And I be pleased to give ten thousand ducats
To have it baned? What, are you answer'd yet?
Some men there are love not a gaping pig;
Some, that are mad if they behold a cat;
And others, when the bagpipe sings i' the nose,
Cannot contain their urine: for affection,
Mistress of passion, sways it to the mood
Of what it likes or loathes. Now, for your answer:
As there is no firm reason to be render'd,
Why he cannot abide a gaping pig;
Why he, a harmless necessary cat;
Why he, a woollen bagpipe; but of force
Must yield to such inevitable shame
As to offend, himself being offended;
So can I give no reason, nor I will not,
More than a lodged hate and a certain loathing
I bear Antonio, that I follow thus
A losing suit against him. Are you answer'd?

BASSANIO
This is no answer, thou unfeeling man,
To excuse the current of thy cruelty.

SHYLOCK
I am not bound to please thee with my answers.

BASSANIO
Do all men kill the things they do not love?

SHYLOCK
Hates any man the thing he would not kill?

BASSANIO
Every offence is not a hate at first.

SHYLOCK
What, wouldst thou have a serpent sting thee twice?

ANTONIO
I pray you, think you question with the Jew:
You may as well go stand upon the beach
And bid the main flood bate his usual height;
You may as well use question with the wolf
Why he hath made the ewe bleat for the lamb;
You may as well forbid the mountain pines
To wag their high tops and to make no noise,
When they are fretten with the gusts of heaven;
You may as well do anything most hard,
As seek to soften that—than which what's harder?—
His Jewish heart: therefore, I do beseech you,
Make no more offers, use no farther means,
But with all brief and plain conveniency
Let me have judgment and the Jew his will.

BASSANIO
For thy three thousand ducats here is six.

SHYLOCK
What judgment shall I dread, doing
Were in six parts and every part a ducat,
I would not draw them; I would have my bond.

DUKE
How shalt thou hope for mercy, rendering none?

SHYLOCK
What judgment shall I dread, doing no wrong?
You have among you many a purchased slave,
Which, like your asses and your dogs and mules,
You use in abject and in slavish parts,
Because you bought them: shall I say to you,
Let them be free, marry them to your heirs?
Why sweat they under burthens? let their beds
Be made as soft as yours and let their palates
Be season'd with such viands? You will answer
'The slaves are ours:' so do I answer you:
The pound of flesh, which I demand of him,
Is dearly bought; 'tis mine and I will have it.
If you deny me, fie upon your law!
There is no force in the decrees of Venice.
I stand for judgment: answer; shall I have it?

DUKE
Upon my power I may dismiss this court,
Unless Bellario, a learned doctor,
Whom I have sent for to determine this,
Come here to-day.

SALERIO
My lord, here stays without
A messenger with letters from the doctor,
New come from Padua.

DUKE
Bring us the letter; call the messenger.

BASSANIO
Good cheer, Antonio! What, man, courage yet!
The Jew shall have my flesh, blood, bones and all,
Ere thou shalt lose for me one drop of blood.

ANTONIO
I am a tainted wether of the flock,
Meetest for death: the weakest kind of fruit
Drops earliest to the ground; and so let me
You cannot better be employ'd, Bassanio,
Than to live still and write mine epitaph.

Enter NERISSA, dressed like a lawyer's clerk

DUKE
Came you from Padua, from Bellario?

NERISSA
From both, my lord. Bellario greets your grace.

Presenting a letter

BASSANIO
Why dost thou whet thy knife so earnestly?

SHYLOCK
To cut the forfeiture from that bankrupt there.

GRATIANO
Not on thy sole, but on thy soul, harsh Jew,
Thou makest thy knife keen; but no metal can,
No, not the hangman's axe, bear half the keenness
Of thy sharp envy. Can no prayers pierce thee?

SHYLOCK
No, none that thou hast wit enough to make.

GRATIANO

O, be thou damn'd, inexecrable dog!
And for thy life let justice be accused.
Thou almost makest me waver in my faith
To hold opinion with Pythagoras,
That souls of animals infuse themselves
Into the trunks of men: thy currish spirit
Govern'd a wolf, who, hang'd for human slaughter,
Even from the gallows did his fell soul fleet,
And, whilst thou lay'st in thy unhallow'd dam,
Infused itself in thee; for thy desires
Are wolvish, bloody, starved and ravenous.

SHYLOCK

Till thou canst rail the seal from off my bond,
Thou but offend'st thy lungs to speak so loud:
Repair thy wit, good youth, or it will fall
To cureless ruin. I stand here for law.

DUKE

This letter from Bellario doth commend
A young and learned doctor to our court.
Where is he?

NERISSA

He attendeth here hard by,
To know your answer, whether you'll admit him.

DUKE

With all my heart. Some three or four of you
Go give him courteous conduct to this place.
Meantime the court shall hear Bellario's letter.

Clerk

[Reads]

Your grace shall understand that at the receipt of your letter I am very sick: but in the instant that your messenger came, in loving visitation was with me a young doctor of Rome; his name is Balthasar. I acquainted him with the cause in controversy between the Jew and Antonio the merchant: we turned o'er many books together: he is furnished with my opinion; which, bettered with his own learning, the greatness whereof I cannot enough commend, comes with him, at my importunity, to fill up your grace's request in my stead. I beseech you, let his lack of years be no impediment to let him lack a reverend estimation; for I never knew so young a body with so old a head. I leave him to your gracious acceptance, whose trial shall better publish his commendation.

DUKE

You hear the learn'd Bellario, what he writes:
And here, I take it, is the doctor come.

Enter PORTIA, dressed like a doctor of laws

Give me your hand. Come you from old Bellario?

PORTIA
I did, my lord.

DUKE
You are welcome: take your place.
Are you acquainted with the difference
That holds this present question in the court?

PORTIA
I am informed thoroughly of the cause.
Which is the merchant here, and which the Jew?

DUKE
Antonio and old Shylock, both stand forth.

PORTIA
Is your name Shylock?

SHYLOCK
Shylock is my name.

PORTIA
Of a strange nature is the suit you follow;
Yet in such rule that the Venetian law
Cannot impugn you as you do proceed.
You stand within his danger, do you not?

ANTONIO
Ay, so he says.

PORTIA
Do you confess the bond?

ANTONIO
I do.

PORTIA
Then must the Jew be merciful.

SHYLOCK
On what compulsion must I? tell me that.

PORTIA
The quality of mercy is not strain'd,
It droppeth as the gentle rain from heaven
Upon the place beneath: it is twice blest;
It blesseth him that gives and him that takes:
'Tis mightiest in the mightiest: it becomes
The throned monarch better than his crown;
His sceptre shows the force of temporal power,

The attribute to awe and majesty,
Wherein doth sit the dread and fear of kings;
But mercy is above this sceptred sway;
It is enthroned in the hearts of kings,
It is an attribute to God himself;
And earthly power doth then show likest God's
When mercy seasons justice. Therefore, Jew,
Though justice be thy plea, consider this,
That, in the course of justice, none of us
Should see salvation: we do pray for mercy;
And that same prayer doth teach us all to render
The deeds of mercy. I have spoke thus much
To mitigate the justice of thy plea;
Which if thou follow, this strict court of Venice
Must needs give sentence 'gainst the merchant there.

SHYLOCK
My deeds upon my head! I crave the law,
The penalty and forfeit of my bond.

PORTIA
Is he not able to discharge the money?

BASSANIO
Yes, here I tender it for him in the court;
Yea, twice the sum: if that will not suffice,
I will be bound to pay it ten times o'er,
On forfeit of my hands, my head, my heart:
If this will not suffice, it must appear
That malice bears down truth. And I beseech you,
Wrest once the law to your authority:
To do a great right, do a little wrong,
And curb this cruel devil of his will.

PORTIA
It must not be; there is no power in Venice
Can alter a decree established:
'Twill be recorded for a precedent,
And many an error by the same example
Will rush into the state: it cannot be.

SHYLOCK
A Daniel come to judgment! yea, a Daniel!
O wise young judge, how I do honour thee!

PORTIA
I pray you, let me look upon the bond.

SHYLOCK
Here 'tis, most reverend doctor, here it is.

PORTIA
Shylock, there's thrice thy money offer'd thee.

SHYLOCK
An oath, an oath, I have an oath in heaven:
Shall I lay perjury upon my soul?
No, not for Venice.

PORTIA
Why, this bond is forfeit;
And lawfully by this the Jew may claim
A pound of flesh, to be by him cut off
Nearest the merchant's heart. Be merciful:
Take thrice thy money; bid me tear the bond.

SHYLOCK
When it is paid according to the tenor.
It doth appear you are a worthy judge;
You know the law, your exposition
Hath been most sound: I charge you by the law,
Whereof you are a well-deserving pillar,
Proceed to judgment: by my soul I swear
There is no power in the tongue of man
To alter me: I stay here on my bond.

ANTONIO
Most heartily I do beseech the court
To give the judgment.

PORTIA
Why then, thus it is:
You must prepare your bosom for his knife.

SHYLOCK
O noble judge! O excellent young man!

PORTIA
For the intent and purpose of the law
Hath full relation to the penalty,
Which here appeareth due upon the bond.

SHYLOCK
'Tis very true: O wise and upright judge!
How much more elder art thou than thy looks!

PORTIA
Therefore lay bare your bosom.

SHYLOCK

Ay, his breast:
So says the bond: doth it not, noble judge?
'Nearest his heart:' those are the very words.

PORTIA
It is so. Are there balance here to weigh
The flesh?

SHYLOCK
I have them ready.

PORTIA
Have by some surgeon, Shylock, on your charge,
To stop his wounds, lest he do bleed to death.

SHYLOCK
Is it so nominated in the bond?

PORTIA
It is not so express'd: but what of that?
'Twere good you do so much for charity.

SHYLOCK
I cannot find it; 'tis not in the bond.

PORTIA
You, merchant, have you any thing to say?

ANTONIO
But little: I am arm'd and well prepared.
Give me your hand, Bassanio: fare you well!
Grieve not that I am fallen to this for you;
For herein Fortune shows herself more kind
Than is her custom: it is still her use
To let the wretched man outlive his wealth,
To view with hollow eye and wrinkled brow
An age of poverty; from which lingering penance
Of such misery doth she cut me off.
Commend me to your honourable wife:
Tell her the process of Antonio's end;
Say how I loved you, speak me fair in death;
And, when the tale is told, bid her be judge
Whether Bassanio had not once a love.
Repent but you that you shall lose your friend,
And he repents not that he pays your debt;
For if the Jew do cut but deep enough,
I'll pay it presently with all my heart.

BASSANIO
Antonio, I am married to a wife
Which is as dear to me as life itself;

But life itself, my wife, and all the world,
Are not with me esteem'd above thy life:
I would lose all, ay, sacrifice them all
Here to this devil, to deliver you.

PORTIA
Your wife would give you little thanks for that,
If she were by, to hear you make the offer.

GRATIANO
I have a wife, whom, I protest, I love:
I would she were in heaven, so she could
Entreat some power to change this currish Jew.

NERISSA
'Tis well you offer it behind her back;
The wish would make else an unquiet house.

SHYLOCK
These be the Christian husbands. I have a daughter;
Would any of the stock of Barrabas
Had been her husband rather than a Christian!

Aside

We trifle time: I pray thee, pursue sentence.

PORTIA
A pound of that same merchant's flesh is thine:
The court awards it, and the law doth give it.

SHYLOCK
Most rightful judge!

PORTIA
And you must cut this flesh from off his breast:
The law allows it, and the court awards it.

SHYLOCK
Most learned judge! A sentence! Come, prepare!

PORTIA
Tarry a little; there is something else.
This bond doth give thee here no jot of blood;
The words expressly are 'a pound of flesh:'
Take then thy bond, take thou thy pound of flesh;
But, in the cutting it, if thou dost shed
One drop of Christian blood, thy lands and goods
Are, by the laws of Venice, confiscate
Unto the state of Venice.

GRATIANO
O upright judge! Mark, Jew: O learned judge!

SHYLOCK
Is that the law?

PORTIA
Thyself shalt see the act:
For, as thou urgest justice, be assured
Thou shalt have justice, more than thou desirest.

GRATIANO
O learned judge! Mark, Jew: a learned judge!

SHYLOCK
I take this offer, then; pay the bond thrice
And let the Christian go.

BASSANIO
Here is the money.

PORTIA
Soft!
The Jew shall have all justice; soft! no haste:
He shall have nothing but the penalty.

GRATIANO
O Jew! an upright judge, a learned judge!

PORTIA
Therefore prepare thee to cut off the flesh.
Shed thou no blood, nor cut thou less nor more
But just a pound of flesh: if thou cut'st more
Or less than a just pound, be it but so much
As makes it light or heavy in the substance,
Or the division of the twentieth part
Of one poor scruple, nay, if the scale do turn
But in the estimation of a hair,
Thou diest and all thy goods are confiscate.

GRATIANO
A second Daniel, a Daniel, Jew!
Now, infidel, I have you on the hip.

PORTIA
Why doth the Jew pause? take thy forfeiture.

SHYLOCK
Give me my principal, and let me go.

BASSANIO

I have it ready for thee; here it is.

PORTIA
He hath refused it in the open court:
He shall have merely justice and his bond.

GRATIANO
A Daniel, still say I, a second Daniel!
I thank thee, Jew, for teaching me that word.

SHYLOCK
Shall I not have barely my principal?

PORTIA
Thou shalt have nothing but the forfeiture,
To be so taken at thy peril, Jew.

SHYLOCK
Why, then the devil give him good of it!
I'll stay no longer question.

PORTIA
Tarry, Jew:
The law hath yet another hold on you.
It is enacted in the laws of Venice,
If it be proved against an alien
That by direct or indirect attempts
He seek the life of any citizen,
The party 'gainst the which he doth contrive
Shall seize one half his goods; the other half
Comes to the privy coffer of the state;
And the offender's life lies in the mercy
Of the duke only, 'gainst all other voice.
In which predicament, I say, thou stand'st;
For it appears, by manifest proceeding,
That indirectly and directly too
Thou hast contrived against the very life
Of the defendant; and thou hast incurr'd
The danger formerly by me rehearsed.
Down therefore and beg mercy of the duke.

GRATIANO
Beg that thou mayst have leave to hang thyself:
And yet, thy wealth being forfeit to the state,
Thou hast not left the value of a cord;
Therefore thou must be hang'd at the state's charge.

DUKE
That thou shalt see the difference of our spirits,
I pardon thee thy life before thou ask it:
For half thy wealth, it is Antonio's;

The other half comes to the general state,
Which humbleness may drive unto a fine.

PORTIA
Ay, for the state, not for Antonio.

SHYLOCK
Nay, take my life and all; pardon not that:
You take my house when you do take the prop
That doth sustain my house; you take my life
When you do take the means whereby I live.

PORTIA
What mercy can you render him, Antonio?

GRATIANO
A halter gratis; nothing else, for God's sake.

ANTONIO
So please my lord the duke and all the court
To quit the fine for one half of his goods,
I am content; so he will let me have
The other half in use, to render it,
Upon his death, unto the gentleman
That lately stole his daughter:
Two things provided more, that, for this favour,
He presently become a Christian;
The other, that he do record a gift,
Here in the court, of all he dies possess'd,
Unto his son Lorenzo and his daughter.

DUKE
He shall do this, or else I do recant
The pardon that I late pronounced here.

PORTIA
Art thou contented, Jew? what dost thou say?

SHYLOCK
I am content.

PORTIA
Clerk, draw a deed of gift.

SHYLOCK
I pray you, give me leave to go from hence;
I am not well: send the deed after me,
And I will sign it.

DUKE
Get thee gone, but do it.

GRATIANO
In christening shalt thou have two god-fathers:
Had I been judge, thou shouldst have had ten more,
To bring thee to the gallows, not the font.

Exit SHYLOCK

DUKE
Sir, I entreat you home with me to dinner.

PORTIA
I humbly do desire your grace of pardon:
I must away this night toward Padua,
And it is meet I presently set forth.

DUKE
I am sorry that your leisure serves you not.
Antonio, gratify this gentleman,
For, in my mind, you are much bound to him.

Exeunt DUKE and his train

BASSANIO
Most worthy gentleman, I and my friend
Have by your wisdom been this day acquitted
Of grievous penalties; in lieu whereof,
Three thousand ducats, due unto the Jew,
We freely cope your courteous pains withal.

ANTONIO
And stand indebted, over and above,
In love and service to you evermore.

PORTIA
He is well paid that is well satisfied;
And I, delivering you, am satisfied
And therein do account myself well paid:
My mind was never yet more mercenary.
I pray you, know me when we meet again:
I wish you well, and so I take my leave.

BASSANIO
Dear sir, of force I must attempt you further:
Take some remembrance of us, as a tribute,
Not as a fee: grant me two things, I pray you,
Not to deny me, and to pardon me.

PORTIA
You press me far, and therefore I will yield.

To ANTONIO

Give me your gloves, I'll wear them for your sake;

To BASSANIO

And, for your love, I'll take this ring from you:
Do not draw back your hand; I'll take no more;
And you in love shall not deny me this.

BASSANIO
This ring, good sir, alas, it is a trifle!
I will not shame myself to give you this.

PORTIA
I will have nothing else but only this;
And now methinks I have a mind to it.

BASSANIO
There's more depends on this than on the value.
The dearest ring in Venice will I give you,
And find it out by proclamation:
Only for this, I pray you, pardon me.

PORTIA
I see, sir, you are liberal in offers
You taught me first to beg; and now methinks
You teach me how a beggar should be answer'd.

BASSANIO
Good sir, this ring was given me by my wife;
And when she put it on, she made me vow
That I should neither sell nor give nor lose it.

PORTIA
That 'scuse serves many men to save their gifts.
An if your wife be not a mad-woman,
And know how well I have deserved the ring,
She would not hold out enemy for ever,
For giving it to me. Well, peace be with you!

Exeunt PORTIA and NERISSA

ANTONIO
My Lord Bassanio, let him have the ring:
Let his deservings and my love withal
Be valued against your wife's commandment.

BASSANIO

Go, Gratiano, run and overtake him;
Give him the ring, and bring him, if thou canst,
Unto Antonio's house: away! make haste.

Exit GRATIANO

Come, you and I will thither presently;
And in the morning early will we both
Fly toward Belmont: come, Antonio.

Exeunt

SCENE II. The Same. A Street.

Enter PORTIA and NERISSA

PORTIA
Inquire the Jew's house out, give him this deed
And let him sign it: we'll away to-night
And be a day before our husbands home:
This deed will be well welcome to Lorenzo.

Enter GRATIANO

GRATIANO
Fair sir, you are well o'erta'en
My Lord Bassanio upon more advice
Hath sent you here this ring, and doth entreat
Your company at dinner.

PORTIA
That cannot be:
His ring I do accept most thankfully:
And so, I pray you, tell him: furthermore,
I pray you, show my youth old Shylock's house.

GRATIANO
That will I do.

NERISSA
Sir, I would speak with you.

Aside to PORTIA

I'll see if I can get my husband's ring,
Which I did make him swear to keep for ever.

PORTIA

[Aside to NERISSA] Thou mayst, I warrant.
We shall have old swearing
That they did give the rings away to men;
But we'll outface them, and outswear them too.

Aloud

Away! make haste: thou knowist where I will tarry.

NERISSA
Come, good sir, will you show me to this house?

Exeunt

ACT V

SCENE I. Belmont. Avenue to Portia's House.

Enter LORENZO and JESSICA

LORENZO
The moon shines bright: in such a night as this,
When the sweet wind did gently kiss the trees
And they did make no noise, in such a night
Troilus methinks mounted the Troyan walls
And sigh'd his soul toward the Grecian tents,
Where Cressid lay that night.

JESSICA
In such a night
Did Thisbe fearfully o'ertrip the dew
And saw the lion's shadow ere himself
And ran dismay'd away.

LORENZO
In such a night
Stood Dido with a willow in her hand
Upon the wild sea banks and waft her love
To come again to Carthage.

JESSICA
In such a night
Medea gather'd the enchanted herbs
That did renew old AEson.

LORENZO
In such a night
Did Jessica steal from the wealthy Jew

And with an unthrift love did run from Venice
As far as Belmont.

JESSICA
In such a night
Did young Lorenzo swear he loved her well,
Stealing her soul with many vows of faith
And ne'er a true one.

LORENZO
In such a night
Did pretty Jessica, like a little shrew,
Slander her love, and he forgave it her.

JESSICA
I would out-night you, did no body come;
But, hark, I hear the footing of a man.

Enter STEPHANO

LORENZO
Who comes so fast in silence of the night?

STEPHANO
A friend.

LORENZO
A friend! what friend? your name, I pray you, friend?

STEPHANO
Stephano is my name; and I bring word
My mistress will before the break of day
Be here at Belmont; she doth stray about
By holy crosses, where she kneels and prays
For happy wedlock hours.

LORENZO
Who comes with her?

STEPHANO
None but a holy hermit and her maid.
I pray you, is my master yet return'd?

LORENZO
He is not, nor we have not heard from him.
But go we in, I pray thee, Jessica,
And ceremoniously let us prepare
Some welcome for the mistress of the house.

Enter LAUNCELOT

LAUNCELOT
Sola, sola! wo ha, ho! sola, sola!

LORENZO
Who calls?

LAUNCELOT
Sola! did you see Master Lorenzo?
Master Lorenzo, sola, sola!

LORENZO
Leave hollaing, man: here.

LAUNCELOT
Sola! where? where?

LORENZO
Here.

LAUNCELOT
Tell him there's a post come from my master, with his horn full of good news: my master will be here
ere morning.

Exit

LORENZO
Sweet soul, let's in, and there expect their coming.
And yet no matter: why should we go in?
My friend Stephano, signify, I pray you,
Within the house, your mistress is at hand;
And bring your music forth into the air.

Exit STEPHANO

How sweet the moonlight sleeps upon this bank!
Here will we sit and let the sounds of music
Creep in our ears: soft stillness and the night
Become the touches of sweet harmony.
Sit, Jessica. Look how the floor of heaven
Is thick inlaid with patines of bright gold:
There's not the smallest orb which thou behold'st
But in his motion like an angel sings,
Still quiring to the young-eyed cherubins;
Such harmony is in immortal souls;
But whilst this muddy vesture of decay
Doth grossly close it in, we cannot hear it.

Enter Musicians

Come, ho! and wake Diana with a hymn!
With sweetest touches pierce your mistress' ear,
And draw her home with music.

Music

JESSICA
I am never merry when I hear sweet music.

LORENZO
The reason is, your spirits are attentive:
For do but note a wild and wanton herd,
Or race of youthful and unhandled colts,
Fetching mad bounds, bellowing and neighing loud,
Which is the hot condition of their blood;
If they but hear perchance a trumpet sound,
Or any air of music touch their ears,
You shall perceive them make a mutual stand,
Their savage eyes turn'd to a modest gaze
By the sweet power of music: therefore the poet
Did feign that Orpheus drew trees, stones and floods;
Since nought so stockish, hard and full of rage,
But music for the time doth change his nature.
The man that hath no music in himself,
Nor is not moved with concord of sweet sounds,
Is fit for treasons, stratagems and spoils;
The motions of his spirit are dull as night
And his affections dark as Erebus:
Let no such man be trusted. Mark the music.

Enter PORTIA and NERISSA

PORTIA
That light we see is burning in my hall.
How far that little candle throws his beams!
So shines a good deed in a naughty world.

NERISSA
When the moon shone, we did not see the candle.

PORTIA
So doth the greater glory dim the less:
A substitute shines brightly as a king
Unto the king be by, and then his state
Empties itself, as doth an inland brook
Into the main of waters. Music! hark!

NERISSA
It is your music, madam, of the house.

PORTIA

Nothing is good, I see, without respect:
Methinks it sounds much sweeter than by day.

NERISSA
Silence bestows that virtue on it, madam.

PORTIA
The crow doth sing as sweetly as the lark,
When neither is attended, and I think
The nightingale, if she should sing by day,
When every goose is cackling, would be thought
No better a musician than the wren.
How many things by season season'd are
To their right praise and true perfection!
Peace, ho! the moon sleeps with Endymion
And would not be awaked.

Music ceases

LORENZO
That is the voice,
Or I am much deceived, of Portia.

PORTIA
He knows me as the blind man knows the cuckoo,
By the bad voice.

LORENZO
Dear lady, welcome home.

PORTIA
We have been praying for our husbands' healths,
Which speed, we hope, the better for our words.
Are they return'd?

LORENZO
Madam, they are not yet;
But there is come a messenger before,
To signify their coming.

PORTIA
Go in, Nerissa;
Give order to my servants that they take
No note at all of our being absent hence;
Nor you, Lorenzo; Jessica, nor you.

A tucket sounds

LORENZO
Your husband is at hand; I hear his trumpet:
We are no tell-tales, madam; fear you not.

PORTIA
This night methinks is but the daylight sick;
It looks a little paler: 'tis a day,
Such as the day is when the sun is hid.

Enter BASSANIO, ANTONIO, GRATIANO, and their followers

BASSANIO
We should hold day with the Antipodes,
If you would walk in absence of the sun.

PORTIA
Let me give light, but let me not be light;
For a light wife doth make a heavy husband,
And never be Bassanio so for me:
But God sort all! You are welcome home, my lord.

BASSANIO
I thank you, madam. Give welcome to my friend.
This is the man, this is Antonio,
To whom I am so infinitely bound.

PORTIA
You should in all sense be much bound to him.
For, as I hear, he was much bound for you.

ANTONIO
No more than I am well acquitted of.

PORTIA
Sir, you are very welcome to our house:
It must appear in other ways than words,
Therefore I scant this breathing courtesy.

GRATIANO
[To NERISSA] By yonder moon I swear you do me wrong;
In faith, I gave it to the judge's clerk:
Would he were gelt that had it, for my part,
Since you do take it, love, so much at heart.

PORTIA
A quarrel, ho, already! what's the matter?

GRATIANO
About a hoop of gold, a paltry ring
That she did give me, whose posy was
For all the world like cutler's poetry
Upon a knife, 'Love me, and leave me not.'

NERISSA

What talk you of the posy or the value?
You swore to me, when I did give it you,
That you would wear it till your hour of death
And that it should lie with you in your grave:
Though not for me, yet for your vehement oaths,
You should have been respective and have kept it.
Gave it a judge's clerk! no, God's my judge,
The clerk will ne'er wear hair on's face that had it.

GRATIANO
He will, an if he live to be a man.

NERISSA
Ay, if a woman live to be a man.

GRATIANO
Now, by this hand, I gave it to a youth,
A kind of boy, a little scrubbed boy,
No higher than thyself; the judge's clerk,
A prating boy, that begg'd it as a fee:
I could not for my heart deny it him.

PORTIA
You were to blame, I must be plain with you,
To part so slightly with your wife's first gift:
A thing stuck on with oaths upon your finger
And so riveted with faith unto your flesh.
I gave my love a ring and made him swear
Never to part with it; and here he stands;
I dare be sworn for him he would not leave it
Nor pluck it from his finger, for the wealth
That the world masters. Now, in faith, Gratiano,
You give your wife too unkind a cause of grief:
An 'twere to me, I should be mad at it.

BASSANIO
[Aside] Why, I were best to cut my left hand off
And swear I lost the ring defending it.

GRATIANO
My Lord Bassanio gave his ring away
Unto the judge that begg'd it and indeed
Deserved it too; and then the boy, his clerk,
That took some pains in writing, he begg'd mine;
And neither man nor master would take aught
But the two rings.

PORTIA
What ring gave you my lord?
Not that, I hope, which you received of me.

BASSANIO
If I could add a lie unto a fault,
I would deny it; but you see my finger
Hath not the ring upon it; it is gone.

PORTIA
Even so void is your false heart of truth.
By heaven, I will ne'er come in your bed
Until I see the ring.

NERISSA
Nor I in yours
Till I again see mine.

BASSANIO
Sweet Portia,
If you did know to whom I gave the ring,
If you did know for whom I gave the ring
And would conceive for what I gave the ring
And how unwillingly I left the ring,
When nought would be accepted but the ring,
You would abate the strength of your displeasure.

PORTIA
If you had known the virtue of the ring,
Or half her worthiness that gave the ring,
Or your own honour to contain the ring,
You would not then have parted with the ring.
What man is there so much unreasonable,
If you had pleased to have defended it
With any terms of zeal, wanted the modesty
To urge the thing held as a ceremony?
Nerissa teaches me what to believe:
I'll die for't but some woman had the ring.

BASSANIO
No, by my honour, madam, by my soul,
No woman had it, but a civil doctor,
Which did refuse three thousand ducats of me
And begg'd the ring; the which I did deny him
And suffer'd him to go displeased away;
Even he that did uphold the very life
Of my dear friend. What should I say, sweet lady?
I was enforced to send it after him;
I was beset with shame and courtesy;
My honour would not let ingratitude
So much besmear it. Pardon me, good lady;
For, by these blessed candles of the night,
Had you been there, I think you would have begg'd
The ring of me to give the worthy doctor.

PORTIA
Let not that doctor e'er come near my house:
Since he hath got the jewel that I loved,
And that which you did swear to keep for me,
I will become as liberal as you;
I'll not deny him any thing I have,
No, not my body nor my husband's bed:
Know him I shall, I am well sure of it:
Lie not a night from home; watch me like Argus:
If you do not, if I be left alone,
Now, by mine honour, which is yet mine own,
I'll have that doctor for my bedfellow.

NERISSA
And I his clerk; therefore be well advised
How you do leave me to mine own protection.

GRATIANO
Well, do you so; let not me take him, then;
For if I do, I'll mar the young clerk's pen.

ANTONIO
I am the unhappy subject of these quarrels.

PORTIA
Sir, grieve not you; you are welcome notwithstanding.

BASSANIO
Portia, forgive me this enforced wrong;
And, in the hearing of these many friends,
I swear to thee, even by thine own fair eyes,
Wherein I see myself—

PORTIA
Mark you but that!
In both my eyes he doubly sees himself;
In each eye, one: swear by your double self,
And there's an oath of credit.

BASSANIO
Nay, but hear me:
Pardon this fault, and by my soul I swear
I never more will break an oath with thee.

ANTONIO
I once did lend my body for his wealth;
Which, but for him that had your husband's ring,
Had quite miscarried: I dare be bound again,
My soul upon the forfeit, that your lord
Will never more break faith advisedly.

PORTIA
Then you shall be his surety. Give him this
And bid him keep it better than the other.

ANTONIO
Here, Lord Bassanio; swear to keep this ring.

BASSANIO
By heaven, it is the same I gave the doctor!

PORTIA
I had it of him: pardon me, Bassanio;
For, by this ring, the doctor lay with me.

NERISSA
And pardon me, my gentle Gratiano;
For that same scrubbed boy, the doctor's clerk,
In lieu of this last night did lie with me.

GRATIANO
Why, this is like the mending of highways
In summer, where the ways are fair enough:
What, are we cuckolds ere we have deserved it?

PORTIA
Speak not so grossly. You are all amazed:
Here is a letter; read it at your leisure;
It comes from Padua, from Bellario:
There you shall find that Portia was the doctor,
Nerissa there her clerk: Lorenzo here
Shall witness I set forth as soon as you
And even but now return'd; I have not yet
Enter'd my house. Antonio, you are welcome;
And I have better news in store for you
Than you expect: unseal this letter soon;
There you shall find three of your argosies
Are richly come to harbour suddenly:
You shall not know by what strange accident
I chanced on this letter.

ANTONIO
I am dumb.

BASSANIO
Were you the doctor and I knew you not?

GRATIANO
Were you the clerk that is to make me cuckold?

NERISSA

Ay, but the clerk that never means to do it,
Unless he live until he be a man.

BASSANIO
Sweet doctor, you shall be my bed-fellow:
When I am absent, then lie with my wife.

ANTONIO
Sweet lady, you have given me life and living;
For here I read for certain that my ships
Are safely come to road.

PORTIA
How now, Lorenzo!
My clerk hath some good comforts too for you.

NERISSA
Ay, and I'll give them him without a fee.
There do I give to you and Jessica,
From the rich Jew, a special deed of gift,
After his death, of all he dies possess'd of.

LORENZO
Fair ladies, you drop manna in the way
Of starved people.

PORTIA
It is almost morning,
And yet I am sure you are not satisfied
Of these events at full. Let us go in;
And charge us there upon inter'gatories,
And we will answer all things faithfully.

GRATIANO
Let it be so: the first inter'gatory
That my Nerissa shall be sworn on is,
Whether till the next night she had rather stay,
Or go to bed now, being two hours to day:
But were the day come, I should wish it dark,
That I were couching with the doctor's clerk.
Well, while I live I'll fear no other thing
So sore as keeping safe Nerissa's ring.

Exeunt

William Shakespeare – A Short Biography

The life of William Shakespeare, arguably the most significant figure in the Western literary canon, is relatively unknown. Even the exact date of his birth is uncertain. April 23rd, the date now generally accepted to be the date of his birth, is a result of a scholarly mistake and the appealing coincidence of its being also the day of his death.

That so little is known about a writer with such great literary scope and accomplishment has naturally invited speculation and conspiracy theories about the authenticity of his authorship, his influence and even his existence.

Shakespeare was born in Stratford-upon-Avon in 1565, possibly on the 23rd April, St. George's Day, and baptised there on 26th April. His father was John Shakespeare, a successful glover and alderman who hailed from Snitterfield. His mother was Mary Arden, whose father was an affluent landowner. In total their union bore eight children; William was the third of these and the eldest surviving son.

Although there is no hard evidence on his education it is widely agreed among scholars that William attended the King's New School in Stratford which was chartered as a free school in 1553. This school was only a quarter of a mile from the house in which he spent his childhood, but since there are no attendance records existing it is assumed, rather than known, this was the base for his education.

Although the quality of education in a grammar school at that time varied wildly the curriculum did not, a key aspect of which, by royal decree, was Latin, and it is undoubtable that the school will have delivered an intensive education in Latin grammar, drawing heavily on the work of the classical Latin authors. If Shakespeare did attend this school then it is very likely the starting point for the fascination with and extensive knowledge of the classical Latin authors which would inform and inspire so much of his work began.

Little more detail is known of William's childhood, or his early teenage years, until, at the age of 18, he married Anne Hathaway, who was 26 and from the nearby village of Shottery. Her father was a yeoman farmer, and their family home a small farmhouse in the village. In his will he left her £6 13s 4d, six pounds, thirteen shillings and fourpence, to be paid on her wedding day. On November 27th, 1582 the consistory court of the Diocese of Worcester issued a marriage licence, and on the 28th two of Hathaway's neighbours, Fulk Sandells and John Richardson, posted bonds which guaranteed that there were no lawful claims to impede the marriage along with a surety of £40 to act as a financial guarantee for the wedding.

The marriage was conducted in some haste since, unusually, the marriage banns were read only once instead of the more normal three times, a decision which would have been taken by the Worcester chancellor. This haste is no doubt due to the child Anne delivered their first child, Susanna, six months later. Susanna, was baptised on May 26th, 1583. Several scholars have voiced their opinion that the wedding was imposed on a reluctant Shakespeare by Hathaway's outraged parents, although, again, there is nothing to formally support the theory. It has been further argued that the circumstances surrounding the wedding, particularly those of the neighbourly assurances, indicate that Shakespeare was involved with two women at the time of his marriage. According to the theory proposed by the early twentieth century scholar Frank Harris, Shakespeare had already chosen to marry a woman named Anne Whateley. It was only once this proposed union became known that Hathaway's outraged family forced him to marry their daughter. Harris goes on to surmise that Shakespeare considered the affair entrapment, and that this led to his wholesale despising of her, a "loathing for his wife [which] was measureless" and which ultimately caused him to leave Stratford and her and make for the theatre. But equally other scholars such as John Aubrey have responded to this with evidence that Shakespeare returned to Stratford every year which, if true, would rather diminish Harris's claim that Hathaway had poisoned Stratford for Shakespeare.

Harris's theory aside, Shakespeare and Hathaway had two more children, twins Hamnet and Judith, baptised on February 2nd,1585. Hamnet, Shakespeare's only son, died during one of the frequent outbreaks of bubonic plague and was buried on the August 11th, 1596, at the age of only eleven.

Little is known of Shakespeare's life during the years following the birth of the twins until he appears mentioned in relation to the London theatres in 1592, apart from a fleeting mention in the complaints bill of a legal case which came before the Queen's Bench court at Westminster, dated Michaelmas Term 1588 and October 9th, 1589. Despite this period of time being referred to in scholarly circles as Shakespeare's "lost years", there are several stories, apocryphal in nature, which are attributed to Shakespeare. For example, there is a legend in Stratford that he fled the town in order to avoid prosecution for poaching deer on the estate of Thomas Lucy, a local squire. It is also supposed that Shakespeare went so far as to take revenge on Lucy, a politician whose Protestantism opposed Shakespeare's Catholic childhood, by writing the following lampooning ballad about him:

> A parliament member, a justice of peace,
> At home a poor scarecrow, at London an ass,
> If lousy is Lucy as some folks miscall it
> Then Lucy is lousy whatever befall it.

However amusing the ballad and legend may be in imagining the life of a young Shakespeare, youthfully mischievous and still developing the wit, sense of adventure and humour which would become integral aspects of his writing, there is simply no evidence either to support the theory or to suggest that Shakespeare penned the ballad. Alongside this are suggestions that he began his theatrical career while minding the horses of the patrons of the London theatres and that he spent some time as a schoolmaster employed by one Alexander Hoghton, a Catholic landowner in Lancashire, in whose will is named "William Shakeshafte". However, this was a popular name in the Lancashire area at that time and there is no evidence that this referred to Shakespeare. The wealth of his writing makes it a frustrating exercise to learn more of his life and the manner in which he achieved those outstanding and lionized works.

Interestingly, the reference to Shakespeare in 1592 which ends the "lost years" is a piece of theatrical criticism by playwright Robert Greene in *Groats-Worth of Wit*. In a scathing passage Greene writes "…there is an upstart Crow, beautified with our feathers, that with his *Tiger's heart wrapped in a Player's hide*, supposes he is as well able to bombast out a blank verse as the best of you: and being an absolute *Johannes factotum*, is in his own conceit the only Shake-scene in a country." From this entry we can make some important inferences which shed light on Shakespeare's career, the first of which is that to be acknowledged, even negatively, by a playwright such as Robert Greene, by this point he must have been making significant impact on the London stage as a writer. Also of significance is the very meaning of the words themselves, for it is generally acknowledged that Shakespeare is being accused of writing with a lofty ambition beyond his capabilities and, more importantly, the capabilities of his contemporaries who were educated at Oxford and Cambridge. Within this remark, then, is an inherent snobbery which Shakespeare would come to resent and ultimately challenge in his writing. Though Greene's parody of "Oh, tiger's heart wrapped in a woman's hide" makes reference to *Henry VI, Part 3*, it is likely that Greene's opinion of Shakespeare was in part informed by another of Shakespeare's plays which was heavily criticised, *Titus Adronicus*, believed to have been written between 1588 and 1593. It was his first attempt at tragedy, almost prototypical, and was written at a time when, according to the scholar Jonathan Bate, he was "experimenting with ways of writing about and representing rape and seduction". Drawing heavily on the sixth book of Ovid's *Metamorphoses* as its main source of inspiration for the rape and mutilation of Lavinia, it offended the sensibilities of the more highbrow members of its audience, whilst presumably also simultaneously intimidating them with its detailed knowledge of Ovid, a writer typically considered the reserve of the university-educated. Not only, then, was Shakespeare demonstrating a knowledge of classical literature which they thought befitted only a traditional scholar and thereby shining a light to the snobbery and exclusivity of such an education, but he was doing it radically and brilliantly.

By 1594 the Lord Chamberlain's Men had recognised his worthiness as a playwright and were performing his works. With the advantage of Shakespeare's progressive writing they rapidly became London's leading company of players, affording him more exposure and, following the death of Queen Elizabeth in 1603, a royal patent by the new king, James I, at which point they changed their name to the King's Men.

Before this success, though, several company members had formed a partnership to build their own theatre which came to be on the south bank of the river Thames, the now-famous and reconstructed Globe theatre. Though it is unclear precisely what Shakespeare's involvement in this venture was, records of his property and investments indicate that he came to be rich during this period, buying the second-largest house in Stratford, called New Place, in 1597, which he made his family home. Prior to this he was living in the parish of St Helen's Bishopsgate, north of the River Thames. He continued to spend most of his time at work in London and from about 1598-1602, he seems to have lived in the Paris Gardens area of Bankside south of the river near The Globe.

Despite efforts to pirate his work, Shakespeare's name was by 1598 so well known that it had already become a selling point in its own right on title pages.

An interesting aside is that theatres were mostly constructed on the south bank of the Thames (then part of the county of Surrey) as performing in London itself was thought to be a bad influence on the masses and subject to periodic bouts of censorship, repression and closing of venues which in the City itself was mainly courtyards and open areas at the many Inns.

Excluded from the City purpose built theatres began to be constructed outside the City limits. This area of the Thames though was rough and naturally vibrant with all sorts of characters, many of them of dubious nature or even criminal. It was also prone, due to its over-crowding and bad sanitation, to bouts of bubonic plague and other diseases particularly during the summer which was a further reason for the theatres there being closed. The Curtain, The Rose, The Swan, The Fortune, The Blackfriars and of course The Globe were all purpose built and situated here, some with an audience capacity approaching 3,000.

The first known printed copies of Shakespeare's plays date from 1594 in quarto editions, though these quarto editions are often considered "bad", a term referring to the likelihood of specific quarto editions being based on, for example, a reconstruction of a play as it was witnessed, rather than Shakespeare's original manuscript. The best example of such memorial reconstruction can be found in the differences between the first and second quarto editions of *Hamlet*. In examining Hamlet's most famous soliloquy, "to be or not to be", we can immediately recognise significant differences. First, the familiar second quarto version:

> To be, or not to be; that is the question:
> Whether 'tis nobler in the mind to suffer
> The slings and arrows of outrageous fortune,
> Or to take arms against a sea of troubles,
> And, by opposing, end them.

And, by contrast, the first quarto version:

> To be, or not to be, I there's the point,
> To Die, to sleep, is that all? I all:

For scholar Henry David Gray the first quarto lines are emblematic of "a distorted version of the completed drama filled out and revised by an inferior poet" and based, he goes on to argue, on the fractured memories of the play as witnessed and performed by the actor playing Marcellus. Gray, and several other critics, consider the first quarto a pirated copy, printed in haste without the writer's permission in an attempt to make quick money following the success of the play in the theatre. In understanding the significance of Marcellus to the theory it is imperative to note that the authenticity of each quarto is based on its similarities to the version of the play found in the first folio, printed in 1623 and believed to be authorised by Shakespeare. Therefore, since in the folio version of *Hamlet* the "to be or not to be" soliloquy is virtually identical to that of the second quarto, it is believed that the second was authored by Shakespeare himself and that the first, by its considerable differences, must therefore be in some way compromised. However, when read in comparison to the folio version, the only character whose lines are almost entirely perfect are those spoken by Marcellus, which, since dramatic practice at the time was for actors to be given only their own lines and three or four word 'cues' based on the lines preceding theirs, suggests that the first quarto is a memorial reconstruction of the play written by the actor who played Marcellus. Having committed his own lines to memory he was able to reproduce them accurately, but was left to fill in the remaining lines and plot from memory which accounts for the truncated and often vastly inferior writing in the first quarto.

According to the remaining cast lists from the period, Shakespeare remained an actor throughout his career as a writer, and it is thought he continued to act after he retired his pen. In 1616 he is recorded in the cast list in Ben Jonson's collected *Works* in the plays *Man in His Humour* 1598) and *Sejanus His Fall* (1603), though some scholars consider his absence from the list of Jonson's *Volpone* evidence that, by 1605, his acting career was nearing its end. Despite this in the First Folio he is listed as one of "the Principle Actors in all these Plays", several of which were only staged after *Volpone*.

By 1604 he had moved again, remaining north of the river, to an area near St. Paul's Cathedral where he rented a fine room amongst fine houses from Christopher Mountjoy, a French hatmaker and Huguenot.

The Anglo-Welsh poet John Davies of Hereford wrote in 1610 that "good Will" tended to play "kingly" roles, suggesting he was still on stage, perhaps now performing the more mature kings such as Lear and Henry VI. There has even been the suggestion that Shakespeare played the ghost of Hamlet's father, though there is little evidence to suggest it.

In 1608 the King's Men purchased the Blackfriars theatre from Henry Evans, and according to Cuthbert Burbage, one of the most highly regarded actors of the time, "placed many players" there "which were Heminges, Condell, Shakespeare, etc." A 1609 lawsuit brought against John Addenbrooke in Stratford on the 7th of June describes Shakespeare as "generosus nuper in curia domini Jacobi" (a gentleman recently at the court of King James) which indicates that by this time he was spending more time in Stratford. A likely cause of this was the bubonic plague, frequent outbreaks of which demanded the equally frequent closing of places of public gathering, principle among which were the theatres. Between May 1603 and February 1610 the theatres were closed for a total of 60 months, meaning there was no acting work and nobody to perform new plays. Though in 1610 Shakespeare returned to Stratford and it is supposed lived with his wife, he made frequent visits to London between 1611-14, being called as a witness in the trial *Bellott v. Mountjoy*, a case addressing concerns about the marriage settlement of Mountjoy's daughter, Mary. In March 1613 he purchased a gatehouse in the former Blackfriars priory, and spent several weeks in the city with his son-in-law John Hall, a physician, married to his daughter Susanna, from November 1614.

No plays are attributed to Shakespeare after 1613, and the last few plays he wrote before this time were in collaboration with other writers, one of whom is likely to be John Fletcher who succeeded him as the house playwright for the King's Men.

In early 1616 his daughter Judith married Thomas Quiney, a vintner and tobacconist. He signed his last will and testament on March 25th, of the same year, and the following day Quiney was ordered to do public penance for having fathered an illegitimate child with a woman named Margaret Wheeler who had died during childbirth which had enabled Quiney to cover up the scandal. This public humiliation would have been embarrassing for Shakespeare and his family.

William Shakespeare died two months later on April 23rd, 1616, survived by his wife and two daughters.

According to his will the bulk of his considerable estate was left to his elder daughter Susanna, with the instruction that she pass it down intact to "the first son of her body". However, though Susanna and Judith had four children between them they all died without progeny, ending Shakespeare's direct lineage. Also in his will was the instruction that his "second best bed" be left to his wife Anne, likely an insult, though the bed was possibly matrimonial and therefore of significant sentimental value.

He was buried two days after his death in the chancel of the Holy Trinity Church in Stratford-Upon-Avon.

The epitaph on the slab which covers his grave includes the following passage,

> Good frend for Iesvs sake forbeare,
> To digg the dvst encloased heare.
> Bleste be ye man yt spares thes stones,
> And cvrst be he yt moves my bones

which, in modern translation, reads

> Good friend, for Jesus's sake forbear,
> To dig the dust enclosed here.
> Blessed be the man that spares these stones,
> And cursed be he that moves my bones.

At some point before 1623 there was a funerary monument erected in his memory on the north wall of Stratford-upon-Avon which features a half-effigy of him writing, and which likens him to Nestor, Socrates and Virgil.

On January 29th, 1741 a white marble memorial statue to him was erected in Poets' Corner in Westminster Abbey.

Though there have been many monuments built around the world in memory of Shakespeare, undoubtedly the greatest memorial of all is the body of work which became the foundation of Western literary canon and an inspiration for every generation.

William Shakespeare – A Concise Bibliography

1589	Comedy of Errors (Comedy)
1590	Henry VI, Part II (History)
	Henry VI, Part III (History)
1591	Henry VI, Part I (History)
1592	Richard III (History)
1593	Taming of the Shrew (Comedy)
	Titus Andronicus (Tragedy)
	Venus and Adonis (Poem)
1594	Rape of Lucrece (Poem)
	Romeo and Juliet (Tragedy)
	Two Gentlemen of Verona (Comedy)
	Love's Labour's Lost (Comedy)
1595	Richard II (History)
	Midsummer Night's Dream (Comedy)
1596	King John (History)
	Merchant of Venice (Comedy)
1597	Henry IV, Part I (History)
	Henry IV, Part II (History)
1598	Passionate Pilgrim (Poem)
	Henry V (History)
	Much Ado about Nothing (Comedy)
1599	Twelfth Night (Comedy)
	As You Like It (Comedy)
	Julius Caesar (Tragedy)
1600	Hamlet (Tragedy)
	Merry Wives of Windsor (Comedy)
1601	Troilus and Cressida (Comedy)
1601	Phoenix and the Turtle (Poem))
1602	All's Well That Ends Well (Comedy)

1604	Othello (Tragedy)
	Measure for Measure
1605	King Lear (Tragedy)
	Macbeth (Tragedy)
1606	Antony and Cleopatra (Tragedy)
1607	Coriolanus (Tragedy)
	Timon of Athens (Tragedy)
1608	Pericles (Comedy)
1609	Cymbeline (Comedy)
	Lover's Complaint (Poem)
1610	Winter's Tale (Comedy)
1611	Tempest (Comedy)
1612	Henry VIII (History)

As regards his 154 sonnets it is almost impossible to date each individually though collectively they were first published in 1609, with two having been published in 1599.

Shakspeare; or, the Poet by Ralph Waldo Emerson

Great (1) men are more distinguished by range and extent than by originality. If we require the originality which consists in weaving, like a spider, their web from their own bowels; in finding clay and making bricks and building the house; no great men are original. Nor does valuable originality consist in unlikeness to other men. The hero is in the press of knights and the thick of events; and seeing what men want and sharing their desire, he adds the needful length of sight and of arm, to come at the desired point. The greatest genius is the most indebted man. A poet is no rattle-brain, saying what comes uppermost, and, because he says every thing, saying at last something good; but a heart in unison with his time and country. There is nothing whimsical and fantastic in his production, but sweet and sad earnest, freighted with the weightiest convictions and pointed with the most determined aim which any man or class knows of in his times. (2)

The Genius of our life is jealous of individuals, and will not have any individual great, except through the general. There is no choice to genius. A great man does not wake up on some fine morning and say, 'I am full of life, I will go to sea and find an Antarctic continent: to-day I will square the circle: I will ransack botany and find a new food for man: I have a new architecture in my mind: I foresee a new mechanic power:' no, but he finds himself in the river of the thoughts and events, forced onward by the ideas and necessities of his contemporaries. (3) He stands where all the eyes of men look one way, and their hands all point in the direction in which he should go. The Church has reared him amidst rites and pomps, and he carries out the advice which her music gave him, and builds a cathedral needed by her chants and processions. He finds a war raging: it educates him, by trumpet, in barracks, and he betters the instruction. He finds two counties groping to bring coal, or flour, or fish, from the place of production to the place of consumption, and he hits on a railroad. Every master has found his materials collected, and his power lay in his sympathy with his people and in his love of the materials he wrought in. What an economy of power! and what a compensation for the shortness of life! All is done to his hand. The world has brought him thus far on his way. The human race has gone out before him, sunk the hills, filled the hollows and bridged the rivers. Men, nations, poets, artisans, women, all have worked for him, and he enters into their labors. Choose any other thing, out of the line of tendency, out of the national feeling and history, and he would have all to do for himself: his powers would be expended in the first preparations. Great genial power, one would almost say, consists in not being original at all; in being altogether receptive; in letting the world do all, and suffering the spirit of the hour to pass unobstructed through the mind. (4)

Shakspeare's youth fell in a time when the English people were importunate for dramatic entertainments. The court took offence easily at political allusions and attempted to suppress them. The Puritans, a growing and energetic party, and the religious among the Anglican church, would suppress them. But the people wanted them. Inn-yards, houses without roofs, and extemporaneous enclosures at country fairs were the ready theatres of strolling players. The people had tasted this new joy; and, as we could not hope to suppress newspapers now,—no, not by the strongest party,— neither then could king, prelate, or puritan, alone or united, suppress an organ which was ballad, epic, newspaper, caucus, lecture, Punch and library, at the same time. Probably king, prelate and puritan, all found their own account in it. It had become, by all causes, a national interest,—by no means conspicuous, so that some great scholar would have thought of treating it in an English history,—but not a whit less considerable because it was cheap and of no account, like a baker's-shop. The best proof of its vitality is the crowd of writers which suddenly broke into this field; Kyd, Marlow, Greene, Jonson, Chapman, Dekker, Webster, Heywood, Middleton, Peele, Ford, Massinger, Beaumont and Fletcher.

The secure possession, by the stage, of the public mind, is of the first importance to the poet who works for it. (5) He loses no time in idle experiments. Here is audience and expectation prepared. In the case of Shakspeare there is much more. At the time when he left Stratford and went up to London, a great body of stage-plays of all dates and writers existed in manuscript and were in turn produced on the boards. Here is the Tale of Troy, which the audience will bear hearing some part of, every week; the Death of Julius Cæsar, and other stories out of Plutarch, which they never tire of; a shelf full of English history, from the chronicles of Brut and Arthur, down to the royal Henries, which men hear eagerly; and a string of doleful tragedies, merry Italian tales and Spanish voyages, which all the London 'prentices know. All the mass has been treated, with more or less skill, by every playwright, and the prompter has the soiled and tattered manuscripts. It is now no longer possible to say who wrote them first. They have been the property of the Theatre so long, and so many rising geniuses have enlarged or altered them, inserting a speech or a whole scene, or adding a song, that no man can any longer claim copyright in this work of numbers. Happily, no man wishes to. They are not yet desired in that way. We have few readers, many spectators and hearers. They had best lie where they are.

Shakspeare, in common with his comrades, esteemed the mass of old plays waste stock, in which any experiment could be freely tried. Had the prestige which hedges about a modern tragedy existed, nothing could have been done. The rude warm blood of the living England circulated in the play, as in street-ballads, and gave body which he wanted to his airy and majestic fancy. The poet needs a ground in popular tradition on which he may work, and which, again, may restrain his art within the due temperance. It holds him to the people, supplies a foundation for his edifice, and in furnishing so much work done to his hand, leaves him at leisure and in full strength for the audacities of his imagination. In short, the poet owes to his legend what sculpture owed to the temple. Sculpture in Egypt and in Greece grew up in subordination to architecture. It was the ornament of the temple wall: at first a rude relief carved on pediments, then the relief became bolder and a head or arm was projected from the wall; the groups being still arranged with reference to the building, which serves also as a frame to hold the figures; and when at last the greatest freedom of style and treatment was reached, the prevailing genius of architecture still enforced a certain calmness and continence in the statue. As soon as the statue was begun for itself, and with no reference to the temple or palace, the art began to decline: freak, extravagance and exhibition took the place of the old temperance. This balance-wheel, which the sculptor found in architecture, the perilous irritability of poetic talent found in the accumulated dramatic materials to which the people were already wonted, and which had a certain excellence which no single genius, however extraordinary, could hope to create.

In point of fact it appears that Shakspeare did owe debts in all directions, and was able to use whatever he found; and the amount of indebtedness may be inferred from Malone's laborious computations in regard to the First, Second and Third parts of Henry VI., in which, "out of 6043 lines, 1771 were written by some author preceding Shakspeare, 2373 by him, on the foundation laid by his predecessors, and 1899 were entirely his own." And the proceeding investigation hardly leaves a single drama of his absolute invention. Malone's sentence is an important piece of external history. In Henry VIII. I think I see plainly the cropping out of the original rock on which his own finer stratum was laid. The first play was written by a superior, thoughtful man, with a vicious ear. I can mark his lines, and know well their cadence. See Wolsey's soliloquy, and the following scene with Cromwell, where instead of the metre of Shakspeare, whose secret is that the thought constructs the tune, so that reading for the sense will best bring out the rhythm,—here the lines are constructed on a given tune, and the verse has even a trace of pulpit eloquence. But the play contains through all its length unmistakable traits of Shakspeare's hand, and some passages, as the account of the coronation, are like autographs. What is odd, the compliment to Queen Elizabeth is in the bad rhythm. (6)

Shakspeare knew that tradition supplies a better fable than any invention can. If he lost any credit of design, he augmented his resources; and, at that day, our petulant demand for originality was not so much pressed. There was no literature for the million. The universal reading, the cheap press, were unknown. A great poet who appears in illiterate times, absorbs into his sphere all the light which is any where radiating. Every intellectual jewel, every flower of sentiment it is his fine office to bring to his people; and he comes to value his memory equally with his invention. (7) He is therefore little solicitous whence his thoughts have been derived; whether through translation, whether through tradition, whether by travel in distant countries, whether by inspiration; from whatever source, they are equally welcome to his uncritical audience. Nay, he borrows very near home. Other men say wise things as well as he; only they say a good many foolish things, and do not know when they have spoken wisely. He knows the sparkle of the true stone, and puts it in high place, wherever he finds it. (8) Such is the happy position of Homer perhaps; of Chaucer, of Saadi. They felt that all wit was their wit. And they are librarians and historiographers, as well as poets. Each romancer was heir and dispenser of all the hundred tales of the world,—

"Presenting Thebes' and Pelops' line
And the tale of Troy divine." (9)

The influence of Chaucer is conspicuous in all our early literature; and more recently not only Pope and Dryden have been beholden to him, but, in the whole society of English writers, a large unacknowledged debt is easily traced. One is charmed with the opulence which feeds so many pensioners. But Chaucer is a huge borrower. Chaucer, it seems, drew continually, through Lydgate and Caxton, from Guido di Colonna, whose Latin romance of the Trojan war was in turn a compilation from Dares Phrygius, Ovid and Statius. Then Petrarch, Boccaccio and the Provençal poets are his benefactors: the Romaunt of the Rose is only judicious translation from William of Lorris and John of Meung: Troilus and Creseide, from Lollius of Urbino: The Cock and the Fox, from the Lais of Marie: The House of Fame, from the French or Italian: and poor Gower he uses as if he were only a brick-kiln or stone-quarry out of which to build his house. (10) He steals by this apology,—that what he takes has no worth where he finds it and the greatest where he leaves it. It has come to be practically a sort of rule in literature, that a man having once shown himself capable of original writing, is entitled thenceforth to steal from the writings of others at discretion. Thought is the property of him who can entertain it and of him who can adequately place it. A certain awkwardness marks the use of borrowed thoughts; but as soon as we have learned what to do with them they become our own.

Thus all originality is relative. Every thinker is retrospective. The learned member of the legislature, at Westminster or at Washington, speaks and votes for thousands. Show us the constituency, and the now invisible channels by which the senator is made aware of their wishes; the crowd of practical and knowing men, who, by correspondence or conversation, are feeding him with evidence, anecdotes and estimates, and it will bereave his fine attitude and resistance of something of their impressiveness. As Sir Robert Peel and Mr. Webster vote, so Locke and Rousseau think, for thousands; and so there were fountains all around Homer, (11) Menu, Saadi, or Milton, from which they drew; friends, lovers, books, traditions, proverbs,—all perished—which, if seen, would go to reduce the wonder. Did the bard speak with authority? Did he feel himself overmatched by any companion? The appeal is to the consciousness of the writer. Is there at last in his breast a Delphi whereof to ask concerning any thought or thing, whether it be verily so, yea or nay? and to have answer, and to rely on that? All the debts which such a man could contract to other wit would never disturb his consciousness of originality; for the ministrations of books and of other minds are a whiff of smoke to that most private reality with which he has conversed. (12)

It is easy to see that what is best written or done by genius in the world, was no man's work, but came by wide social labor, when a thousand wrought like one, sharing the same impulse. Our English Bible is a wonderful specimen of the strength and music of the English language. But it was not made by one man, or at one time; but centuries and churches brought it to perfection. There never was a time when there was not some translation existing. The Liturgy, admired for its energy and pathos, is an anthology of the piety of ages and nations, a translation of the prayers and forms of the Catholic church,—these collected, too, in long periods, from the prayers and meditations of every saint and sacred writer all over the world. (13) Grotius makes the like remark in respect to the Lord's Prayer, that the single clauses of which it is composed were already in use in the time of Christ, in the Rabbinical forms. He picked out the grains of gold. The nervous language of the Common Law, the impressive forms of our courts and the precision and substantial truth of the legal distinctions, are the contribution of all the sharp-sighted, strong-minded men who have lived in the countries where these laws govern. The translation of Plutarch gets its excellence by being translation on translation. There never was a time when there was none. All the truly idiomatic and national phrases are kept, and all others successively picked out and thrown away. Something like the same process had gone on, long before, with the originals of these books. The world takes liberties with world-books. Vedas, Æsop's Fables, Pilpay, Arabian Nights, Cid, Iliad, Robin Hood, Scottish Minstrelsy, are not the work of single men. In the composition of such works the time thinks, the market thinks, the mason, the carpenter, the merchant, the farmer, the fop, all think for us. Every book supplies its time with one good word; every municipal law, every trade, every folly of the day; and the generic catholic genius who is not afraid or ashamed to owe his originality to the originality of all, stands with the next age as the recorder and embodiment of his own. (14)

We have to thank the researches of antiquaries, and the Shakspeare Society, for ascertaining the steps of the English drama, from the Mysteries celebrated in churches and by churchmen, and the final detachment from the church, and the completion of secular plays, from Ferrex and Porrex, (15) and Gammer Gurton's Needle, down to the possession of the stage by the very pieces which

Shakspeare altered, remodelled and finally made his own. Elated with success and piqued by the growing interest of the problem, they have left no bookstall unsearched, no chest in a garret unopened, no file of old yellow accounts to decompose in damp and worms, so keen was the hope to discover whether the boy Shakspeare poached or not, whether he held horses at the theatre door, whether he kept school, and why he left in his will only his second-best bed to Ann Hathaway, his wife.

There is somewhat touching in the madness with which the passing age mischooses the object on which all candles shine and all eyes are turned; the care with which it registers every trifle touching Queen Elizabeth and King James, and the Essexes, Leicesters, Burleighs and Buckinghams; and lets pass without a single valuable note the founder of another dynasty, which alone will cause the Tudor dynasty to be remembered,—the man who carries the Saxon race in him by the inspiration which feeds him, and on whose thoughts the foremost people of the world are now for some ages to be nourished, and minds to receive this and not another bias. A popular player;—nobody suspected he was the poet of the human race; and the secret was kept as faithfully from poets and intellectual men as from courtiers and frivolous people. (16) Bacon, who took the inventory of the human understanding for his times, never mentioned his name. Ben Jonson, though we have strained his few words of regard and panegyric, had no suspicion of the elastic fame whose first vibrations he was attempting. He no doubt thought the praise he has conceded to him generous, and esteemed himself, out of all question, the better poet of the two.

If it need wit to know wit, according to the proverb, Shakspeare's time should be capable of recognizing it. Sir Henry Wotton was born four years after Shakspeare, and died twenty-three years after him; and I find, among his correspondents and acquaintances, the following persons: Theodore Beza, Isaac Casaubon, Sir Philip Sidney, the Earl of Essex, Lord Bacon, Sir Walter Raleigh, John Milton, Sir Henry Vane, Isaac Walton, Dr. Donne, Abraham Cowley, Bellarmine, Charles Cotton, John Pym, John Hales, Kepler, Vieta, Albericus Gentilis, Paul Sarpi, Arminius; with all of whom exists some token of his having communicated, without enumerating many others whom doubtless he saw,— Shakspeare, Spenser, Jonson, Beaumont, Massinger, the two Herberts, Marlow, Chapman and the rest. Since the constellation of great men who appeared in Greece in the time of Pericles, there was never any such society;—yet their genius failed them to find out the best head in the universe. (17) Our poet's mask was impenetrable. You cannot see the mountain near. It took a century to make it suspected; and not until two centuries had passed, after his death, did any criticism which we think adequate begin to appear. It was not possible to write the history of Shakspeare till now; for he is the father of German literature: it was with the introduction of Shakspeare into German, by Lessing, and the translation of his works by Wieland and Schlegel, that the rapid burst of German literature was most intimately connected. It was not until the nineteenth century, whose speculative genius is a sort of living Hamlet, that the tragedy of Hamlet could find such wondering readers. (18) Now, literature, philosophy and thought are Shakspearized. His mind is the horizon beyond which, at present, we do not see. Our ears are educated to music by his rhythm. Coleridge and Goethe are the only critics who have expressed our convictions with any adequate fidelity: but there is in all cultivated minds a silent appreciation of his superlative power and beauty, which, like Christianity, qualifies the period.

The Shakspeare Society have inquired in all directions, advertised the missing facts, offered money for any information that will lead to proof,—and with what result? Beside some important illustration of the history of the English stage, to which I have adverted, they have gleaned a few facts touching the property, and dealings in regard to property, of the poet. It appears that from year to year he owned a larger share in the Blackfriars' Theatre: its wardrobe and other appurtenances were his: that he bought an estate in his native village with his earnings as writer and shareholder; that he lived in the best house in Stratford; was intrusted by his neighbors with their commissions in London, as of borrowing money, and the like; that he was a veritable farmer. About the time when he was writing Macbeth, he sues Philip Rogers, in the borough-court of Stratford, for thirty-five shillings, ten pence, for corn delivered to him at different times; and in all respects appears as a good husband, with no reputation for eccentricity or excess. He was a good-natured sort of man, an actor and shareholder in the theatre, not in any striking manner distinguished from other actors and managers. (19) I admit the importance of this information. It was well worth the pains that have been taken to procure it.

But whatever scraps of information concerning his condition these researches may have rescued, they can shed no light upon that infinite invention which is the concealed magnet of his attraction for us. We are very clumsy writers of history. We tell the chronicle of parentage, birth, birth-place, schooling, school-mates, earning of money, marriage, publication of books, celebrity, death; and when we have come to an end of this gossip, no ray of relation appears between it and the goddess-born; and it seems as if, had we dipped at random into the "Modern Plutarch," and read any other life there, it would have fitted the poems as well. (20) It is the essence of poetry to spring, like the rainbow daughter of Wonder, from the invisible, to abolish the past and refuse all history. Malone, Warburton, Dyce and Collier have wasted their oil. The famed theatres, Covent Garden, Drury Lane, the Park and Tremont have vainly assisted. Betterton, Garrick, Kemble, Kean and Macready dedicate their lives to this genius; him they crown, elucidate, obey and express. The genius knows them not. The recitation begins; one golden word leaps out immortal from all this painted pedantry and sweetly torments us with invitations to its own inaccessible homes. I remember I went once to see the Hamlet of a famed performer, the pride of the English stage; and all I then heard and all I now remember of the tragedian was that in which the tragedian had no part; simply Hamlet's question to the ghost:—

"What may this mean,
That thou, dead corse, again in complete steel
Revisit'st thus the glimpses of the moon?"

That imagination which dilates the closet he writes in to the world's dimension, crowds it with agents in rank and order, as quickly reduces the big reality to be the glimpses of the moon. (21) These tricks of his magic spoil for us the illusions of the green-room. Can any biography shed light on the localities into which the Midsummer Night's Dream admits me? Did Shakspeare confide to any notary or parish recorder, sacristan, or surrogate in Stratford, the genesis of that delicate creation? The forest of Arden, the nimble air of Scone Castle, the moonlight of Portia's villa, "the antres vast and desarts idle" of Othello's captivity,—where is the third cousin, or grand-nephew, the chancellor's file of accounts, or private letter, that has kept one word of those transcendent secrets? In fine, in this drama, as in all great works of art,—in the Cyclopæan architecture of Egypt and India, in the Phidian sculpture, the Gothic minsters, the Italian painting, the Ballads of Spain and Scotland,—the Genius draws up the ladder after him, when the creative age goes up to heaven, and gives way to a new age, which sees the works and asks in vain for a history.

Shakspeare is the only biographer of Shakspeare; and even he can tell nothing, except to the Shakspeare in us, that is, to our most apprehensive and sympathetic hour. (22) He cannot step from off his tripod and give us anecdotes of his inspirations. Read the antique documents extricated, analyzed and compared by the assiduous Dyce and Collier, and now read one of these skyey sentences,—aerolites,—which seem to have fallen out of heaven, and which not your experience but the man within the breast has accepted as words of fate, and tell me if they match; if the former account in any manner for the latter; or which gives the most historical insight into the man.

Hence, though our external history is so meagre, yet, with Shakspeare for biographer, instead of Aubrey and Rowe, we have really the information which is material; that which describes character and fortune, that which, if we were about to meet the man and deal with him, would most import us to know. We have his recorded convictions on those questions which knock for answer at every heart,—on life and death, on love, on wealth and poverty, on the prizes of life and the ways whereby we come at them; on the characters of men, and the influences, occult and open, which affect their fortunes; and on those mysterious and demoniacal powers which defy our science and which yet interweave their malice and their gift in our brightest hours. Who ever read the volume of the Sonnets without finding that the poet had there revealed, under masks that are no masks to the intelligent, the lore of friendship and of love; the confusion of sentiments in the most susceptible, and, at the same time, the most intellectual of men? What trait of his private mind has he hidden in his dramas? One can discern, in his ample pictures of the gentleman and the king, what forms and humanities pleased him; his delight in troops of friends, in large hospitality, in cheerful giving. Let Timon, let Warwick, let Antonio the merchant answer for his great heart. So far from Shakspeare's being the least known, he is the one person, in all modern history, known to us. What point of morals, of manners, of economy, of philosophy, of religion, of taste, of the conduct of life, has he not settled? What mystery has he not signified his knowledge of? What office, or function, or district of man's work, has he not remembered? What king has he not taught state, as Talma taught Napoleon? What maiden has not found him finer than her delicacy? What lover has he not outloved? What sage has he not outseen? What gentleman has he not instructed in the rudeness of his behavior?

Some able and appreciating critics think no criticism on Shakspeare valuable that does not rest purely on the dramatic merit; that he is falsely judged as poet and philosopher. I think as highly as these critics of his dramatic merit, but still think it secondary. He was a full man, who liked to talk; a brain exhaling thoughts and images, which, seeking vent, found the drama next at hand. (23) Had he been less, we should have had to consider how well he filled his place, how good a dramatist he was,—and he is the best in the world. But it turns out that what he has to say is of that weight as to withdraw some attention from the vehicle; and he is like some saint whose history is to be rendered into all languages, into verse and prose, into songs and pictures, and cut up into proverbs; so that the occasion which gave the saint's meaning the form of a conversation, or of a prayer, or of a code of laws, is immaterial compared with the universality of its application. So it fares with the wise Shakspeare and his book of life. He wrote the airs for all our modern music: he wrote the text of modern life; the text of manners: he drew the man of England and Europe; the father of the man in America; (24) he drew the man, and described the day, and what is done in it: he read the hearts of men and women, their probity, and their second thought and wiles; the wiles of innocence, and the transitions by which virtues and vices slide into their contraries: he could divide the mother's part from the father's part in the face of the child, or draw the fine demarcations of freedom and of fate: he knew the laws of repression which make the police of nature: and all the sweets and all the terrors of human lot lay in his mind as truly but as softly as the landscape lies on the eye. And the importance of this wisdom of life sinks the form, as of Drama or Epic, out of notice. 'T is like making a question concerning the paper on which a king's message is written.

Shakspeare is as much out of the category of eminent authors, as he is out of the crowd. He is inconceivably wise; the others, conceivably. A good reader can, in a sort, nestle into Plato's brain and think from thence; but not into Shakspeare's. We are still out of doors. For executive faculty, for creation, Shakspeare is unique. No man can imagine it better. He was the farthest reach of subtlety compatible with an individual self,—the subtlest of authors, and only just within the possibility of authorship. (25) With this wisdom of life is the equal endowment of imaginative and of lyric power. He clothed the creatures of his legend with form and sentiments as if they were people who had lived under his roof; and few real men have left such distinct characters as these fictions. And they spoke in language as sweet as it was fit. Yet his talents never seduced him into an ostentation, nor did he harp on one string. An omnipresent humanity co-ordinates all his faculties. Give a man of talents a story to tell, and his partiality will presently appear. He has certain observations, opinions, topics, which have some accidental prominence, and which he disposes all to exhibit. He crams this part and starves that other part, consulting not the fitness of the thing, but his fitness and strength. But Shakspeare has no peculiarity, no importunate topic; but all is duly given; no veins, no curiosities; no cow-painter, no bird-fancier, no mannerist is he: he has no discoverable egotism: the great he tells greatly; the small subordinately. He is wise without emphasis or assertion; he is strong, as nature is strong, who lifts the land into mountain slopes without effort and by the same rule as she floats a bubble in the air, and likes as well to do the one as the other. This makes that equality of power in farce, tragedy, narrative, and love-songs; a merit so incessant that each reader is incredulous of the perception of other readers.

This power of expression, or of transferring the inmost truth of things into music and verse, makes him the type of the poet and has added a new problem to metaphysics. This is that which throws him into natural history, as a main production of the globe, and as announcing new eras and ameliorations. Things were mirrored in his poetry without loss or blur: he could paint the fine with precision, the great with compass, the tragic and the comic indifferently and without any distortion or favor. He carried his powerful execution into minute details, to a hair point; finishes an eyelash or a dimple as firmly as he draws a mountain; and yet these, like nature's, will bear the scrutiny of the solar microscope.

In short, he is the chief example to prove that more or less of production, more or fewer pictures, is a thing indifferent. He had the power to make one picture. Daguerre learned how to let one flower etch its image on his plate of iodine, and then proceeds at leisure to etch a million. There are always objects; but there was never representation. Here is perfect representation, at last; and now let the world of figures sit for their portraits. No recipe can be given for the making of a Shakspeare; but the possibility of the translation of things into song is demonstrated.

His lyric power lies in the genius of the piece. The sonnets, though their excellence is lost in the splendor of the dramas, are as inimitable as they; and it is not a merit of lines, but a total merit of the piece; like the tone of voice of some incomparable person, so is this a speech of poetic beings, and any clause as unproducible now as a whole poem.

Though the speeches in the plays, and single lines, have a beauty which tempts the ear to pause on them for their euphuism, yet the sentence is so loaded with meaning and so linked with its foregoers and followers, that the logician is satisfied. His means are as admirable as his ends; every subordinate invention, by which he helps himself to connect some irreconcilable opposites, is a poem too. He is not reduced to dismount and walk because his horses are running off with him in some distant direction: he always rides.

The finest poetry was first experience; but the thought has suffered a transformation since it was an experience. Cultivated men often attain a good degree of skill in writing verses; but it is easy to read, through their poems, their personal history: any one acquainted with the parties can name every figure; this is Andrew and that is Rachel. The sense thus remains prosaic. It is a caterpillar with wings, and not yet a butterfly. In the poet's mind the fact has gone quite over into the new element of thought, and has lost all that is exuvial. This generosity abides with Shakespeare. We say, from the truth and closeness of his pictures, that he knows the lesson by heart. Yet there is not a trace of egotism.

One more royal trait properly belongs to the poet. I mean his cheerfulness, without which no man can be a poet,—for beauty is his aim. He loves virtue, not for its obligation but for its grace: he delights in the world, in man, in woman, for the lovely light that sparkles from them. Beauty, the spirit of joy and hilarity, he sheds over the universe. Epicurus relates that poetry hath such charms that a lover might forsake his mistress to partake of them. And the true bards have been noted for their firm and cheerful temper. Homer lies in sunshine; Chaucer is glad and erect; and Saadi says, "It was rumored abroad that I was penitent; but what had I to do with repentance?" (26) Not less sovereign and cheerful,—much more sovereign and cheerful, is the tone of Shakespeare. His name suggests joy and emancipation to the heart of men. If he should appear in any company of human souls, who would not march in his troop? He touches nothing that does not borrow health and longevity from his festal style.

And now, how stands the account of man with this bard and benefactor, when, in solitude, shutting our ears to the reverberations of his fame, we seek to strike the balance? Solitude has austere lessons; it can teach us to spare both heroes and poets; and it weighs Shakespeare also, and finds him to share the halfness and imperfection of humanity.

Shakespeare, Homer, Dante, Chaucer, saw the splendor of meaning that plays over the visible world; knew that a tree had another use than for apples, and corn another than for meal, and the ball of the earth, than for tillage and roads: that these things bore a second and finer harvest to the mind, being emblems of its thoughts, and conveying in all their natural history a certain mute commentary on human life. (27) Shakespeare employed them as colors to compose his picture. He rested in their beauty; and never took the step which seemed inevitable to such genius, namely to explore the virtue which resides in these symbols and imparts this power:—what is that which they themselves say? He converted the elements which waited on his command, into entertainments. He was master of the revels to mankind. Is it not as if one should have, through majestic powers of science, the comets given into his hand, or the planets and their moons, and should draw them from their orbits to glare with the municipal fireworks on a holiday night, and advertise in all towns, "Very superior pyrotechny this evening"? Are the agents of nature, and the power to understand them, worth no more than a street serenade, or the breath of a cigar? One remembers again the trumpet-text in the Koran,—"The heavens and the earth and all that is between them, think ye we have created them in jest?" As long as the question is of talent and mental power, the world of men has not his equal to show. But when the question is, to life and its materials and its auxiliaries, how does he profit me? What does it signify? It is but a Twelfth Night, or Midsummer-Night's Dream, or Winter Evening's Tale: what signifies another picture more or less? The Egyptian verdict of the Shakespeare Societies comes to mind; that he was a jovial actor and manager. I can not marry this fact to his verse. Other admirable men have led lives in some sort of keeping with their thought; but this man, in wide contrast. Had he been less, had he reached only the common measure of great authors, of Bacon, Milton, Tasso, Cervantes, we might leave the fact in the twilight of human fate: but that this man of men, he who gave to the science of mind a new and larger subject than had ever existed, and planted the standard of humanity some furlongs forward into Chaos,—that he should not be wise for himself;—it must even go into the world's history that the best poet led an obscure and profane life, using his genius for the public amusement. (28)

Well, other men, priest and prophet, Israelite, German and Swede, beheld the same objects: they also saw through them that which was contained. And to what purpose? The beauty straightway vanished; they read commandments, all-excluding mountainous duty; an obligation, a sadness, as of piled mountains, fell on them, and life became ghastly, joyless, a pilgrim's progress, a probation, beleaguered round with doleful histories of Adam's fall and curse behind us; with doomsdays and purgatorial and penal fires before us; and the heart of the seer and the heart of the listener sank in them.

It must be conceded that these are half-views of half-men. The world still wants its poet-priest, a reconciler, who shall not trifle, with Shakespeare the player, nor shall grope in graves, with Swedenborg the mourner; but who shall see, speak, and act, with equal inspiration. For knowledge will brighten the sunshine; right is more beautiful than private affection; and love is compatible with universal wisdom. (29)

Footnotes

Note 1.

This essay was read as a lecture in Exeter Hall, in London, in June, 1848.

Perhaps it is well to bear in mind that Mr. Emerson was reared for the ministry and ordained a clergyman, and that his ancestors for several generations had exercised that office, and moreover that, in New England, up to his day, theatrical representations had been looked at with disfavor by serious and God-fearing people, and the witnessing of such by a minister would, like dancing, have been considered unbecoming indulgence. Although Mr. Emerson emancipated himself from bonds that were merely professional or artificial, he had an inbred distaste for the common amusements of society, feeling that they were unbecoming to a scholar, and that he was not adapted for them, though he was tolerant of them in other people. There was a natural earnestness, and a simple and cheerful asceticism in his early and later life. Yet once in his later life, when he had been induced to go to see Mr. and Mrs. Barney Williams in some bright comedy, he praised their acting and admitted to his daughter that he really much enjoyed theatrical performances, in spite of the feeling that they were not for him. Dancing, for instance, which he considered a proper part of youths' education, would have seemed unbecoming for himself. He says, "It shall be writ in my memoirs ... as it was writ of St. Pachonius, Pes ejus ad saltandum non est commotus omni vita sua." His staying away from theatrical entertainments was instinctive, but he was liberal in the matter and would go to see a real artist. He even went to see the performance of the beautiful dancer Fanny Elssler, although a story which has been too often repeated of his remarks to Margaret Fuller on the subject is as false as it is silly.

In Paris he saw Rachel during the Revolution of 1848, and often told his children of her fierce and splendid declamation of the Marseillaise in the theatre, holding the tricolor aloft. On London in that same year he wrote of seeing Macready in Lear, with Mrs. Butler as Cordelia. It was to see one of Shakspeare's heroes rendered by some master that he went, and probably he never was inside a theatre twenty times in his life, and, so sensitive was he to had taste or ranting, that he was usually sorry that had gone.

The rendering of Richard II. (I cannot remember by whom) more than satisfied him, and he liked to recall the actor's tones in reading this play, an especial favorite of his, to his children. Coriolanus and Julius Cæsar too he enjoyed reading to them, and he selected passages from Shakspeare for them and trained them very carefully for their recitation in school.

He saw Edwin Booth in Boston, and met him later at the house of a friend and had some talk with him. Booth later mentioned with pleasure to their host the fact that Mr. Emerson had not once alluded to his profession or performance in their conversation.

Mr. Emerson once defined the cultivated man as "one who can tell you something new and true about Shakspeare." And he read a good omen for our age in Shakspeare's acceptance: "The book only characterizes the reader. Is Shakspeare the delight of the nineteenth century? That fact only shows whereabouts we are in the ecliptic of the soul."

In writing of Great Men in 1838 in his journal, he says:—

"Swedenborg is scarce yet appreciable. Shakspeare has, for the first time, in our time found adequate criticism, if indeed he have yet found it:—Coleridge, Lamb, Schlegel, Goethe, Very, Herder.

"The great facts of history are four or five names, Homer—Phidias—Jesus—Shakspeare. One or two names more I will not add, but see what these names stand for. All civil history and all philosophy consists of endeavours more or less vain to explain these persons."

In the journal for 1843 he writes: "Plato is weak inasmuch as he is literary. Shakspeare is not literary, but the strong earth itself." Yet from another point of view he writes, "Shakspeare and Plato each sufficed for the culture of a nation."

That Shakspeare and Milton should have been born meant much to him and to mankind. "Who saw Milton, who saw Shakspeare, saw them do their best, and utter their whole heart manlike among their contemporaries."

And again, "No man can be named whose mind still acts on the cultivated intellect of England and America with an energy comparable to that of Milton. As a poet, Shakspeare undoubtedly transcends and far surpasses him in his popularity with foreign nations: but Shakspeare is a voice merely: who and what he was that sang, that sings, we know not."

Note 2.

Mr. Emerson said of Nature:—

No ray is dimmed, no atom worn,
My oldest force is good as new,
And the fresh rose on yonder thorn
Gives back the bending heavens in dew;—

and her cheerful lesson for the artist or poet was that he too could forever re-combine the old material into fresh and splendid pictures. He rejoiced that "the poet is permitted to dip his brush into the old paint-pot with which birds, flowers, the human cheek, the living rock, the broad landscape, the ocean and the eternal sky were painted," and turning from the reading of the plays he says: "'T is Shakspeare's fault that the world appears so empty. He has educated you with his painted world, and this real one seems a huckster's-shop." Again as to his true rendering of men's characters, "I value Shakspeare as a metaphysician and admire the unspoken logic which upholds the structure of Iago, Macbeth, Antony and the rest."

Note 3.

Again the ancient doctrine of the Flowing, and the modern onward and upward stream of Evolution.

Note 4.

The passive Master lent his hand
To the vast soul that o'er him planned.

"The Problem," Poems.

Note 5.

The stage was to Shakspeare his opportunity, as the Lyceum was to Emerson.

Note 6.

Henry VIII., Act V., Scene iv.

Note 7.

This estimate of the value of memory to the poet, typified by the Greeks in their making the Muses the daughters of Mnemosyne, is enlarged upon in the Essay on "Memory" in Natural History of Intellect. Mr. Emerson said once, "Of the most romantic fact the memory is more romantic," and he quotes Quintilian as saying, Quantum ingenii, tantum memoriæ.

Note 8.

In a fragment of verse written in Mr. Emerson's journal of 1831 on the yearning of the poet to enrich himself from the Treasury of the Universe, he says:—

And if to me it is not given
To fetch one ingot thence
Of that unfading gold of Heaven
His merchants may dispense,
Yet well I know the royal mine,

And know the sparkle of its ore,
Know Heaven's truth from lies that shine,—

Explored, they teach us to explore.
"Fragments on the Poet," Poems, Appendix.

Note 9.

Milton, "Il Penseroso."

Note 10.

Taine, in his History of English Literature, thus justifies Chaucer's borrowing or rendering:—

"Chaucer was capable of seeking out, in the old common forest of the middle ages, stories and legends, to replant them in his own soil and make them send out new shoots.... He has the right and power of copying and translating because by dint of retouching he impresses ... his original mark. He re-creates what he imitates.... At the distance of a century and a half he has affinity with the poets of Elizabeth by his gallery of pictures."

The dates of Lydgate and Caxton show a mistake as to his use of them. Caxton, following Chaucer, when he introduced the printing-press to England, printed his poems and those of Lydgate, who was younger than Chaucer. In his House of Fame, Chaucer places, in his vision, "on a pillar higher than the rest, Homer and Livy, Dares the Phrygian, Guido Colonna, Geoffrey of Monmouth and the other historians of the war of Troy" [Taine's History of English Literature], a due recognition of his debt for Troylus and Cryseyde. As for Gower, he was Chaucer's exact contemporary and friend, and Chaucer dedicated this poem to him.

Note 11.

Kipling irreverently tells of Homer's borrowings thus:—

"When 'Omer smote 'is bloomin' lyre,
He 'd 'eard men sing by land an' sea;
An' what he thought 'e might require,
'E went an' took—the same as me!"
And says of his humble audience:—

"They knew 'e stole; 'e knew they knowed.
They did n't tell, nor make a fuss,
But winked at 'Omer down the road,
An' 'e winked back—the same as us!"

Note 12.

Dr. Holmes's remark with regard to the preceding page is: "The reason why Emerson has so much to say on this subject of borrowing, especially when treating of Plato and Shakspeare, is obvious enough. He was arguing his own cause—not defending himself," etc. In Letters and Social Aims, Mr. Emerson discusses Quotation and Originality.

Note 13.

Mr. Emerson had tender associations with the Book of Common Prayer. His mother had been brought up in the Episcopal communion, and the prayer-book of her youth was always by her, though after her marriage she attended her husband's church. [In Mr. Cabot's Memoir, vol. ii. p. 572, see Mr. Emerson's letter on his mother's death.]

Note 14.

Landor says of these borrowings of Shakspeare, "He breathed upon dead bodies and brought them to life."

Note 15.

The princes Ferrex and Porrex, brothers and rivals for the ancient British throne, are characters in the tragedy Gorboduc by Norton and Sackville, to which the date 1561 is assigned. Gammer Gurton's Needle is a comedy of the same period.

Note 16.

Journal, 1864. "Shakspeare puts us all out. No theory will account for him. He neglected his works, perchance he did not know their value? Ay, but he did; witness the sonnets. He went into company as a listener, hiding himself, [Greek]; was only remembered by all as a delightful companion."

Note 17.

England's genius filled all measure
Of heart and soul, of strength and pleasure,
Gave to the mind its emperor,
And life was larger than before:
Nor sequent centuries could hit
Orbit and sum of Shakspeare's wit.
The men who lived with him became
Poets, for the air was fame.
"The Solution," Poems.

Note 18.

While writing this, Mr. Emerson was surrounded by persons paralyzed for active life in the common world by the doubts of conscience or entangled in over-fine-spun webs of their intellect. [back]

Note 19.

Journal, 1837. "I either read or inferred to-day in the Westminster Review that Shakspeare was not a popular man in his day. How true and wise. He sat alone and walked alone, a visionary poet, and came with his piece, modest but discerning, to the players, and was too glad to get it received, whilst he was too superior not to see its transcendent claims."

Note 20.

The following is the "Exordium of a lecture on Poetry and Eloquence," given in London in 1848:

"Shakspeare is nothing but a large utterance. We cannot find that anything in his age was more worth telling than anything in ours; nor give any account of his existence, but only the fact that there was a wonderful symbolizer and expresser, who has no rival in the ages, and who has thrown an accidental lustre over his time and subject."

In the lecture on "Works and Days" he wrote, "Shakspeare made his Hamlet as a bird weaves its nest." And in that on "Inspiration" in Letters and Social Aims: "Shakspeare seems to you miraculous, but the wonderful juxtapositions, parallelisms, transfers, which his genius effected, were all to him locked together as links of a chain, and the mode precisely as conceivable and familiar to higher intelligence as the index-making of the literary hack."

Journal, 1838. "Read Lear yesterday and Hamlet to-day with new wonder and mused much on the great Soul in the broad continuous daylight of these poems. Especially I wonder at the perfect reception this wit and immense knowledge of life and intellectual superiority find in us all in connection with our utter incapacity to produce anything like it. The superior tone of Hamlet in all the conversations how perfectly preserved, without any mediocrity, much less any dulness in the other speakers.

"How real the loftiness! an inborn gentleman; and above that, an exalted intellect. What incessant growth and plenitude of thought,—pausing on itself never an instant, and each sally of wit sufficient to save the play. How true then and unerring the earnest of the dialogue, as when Hamlet talks with the Queen. How terrible his discourse! What less can be said of the perfect mastery, as by a superior being, of the conduct of the drama, as the free introduction of this capital advice to the players; the

commanding good sense which never retreats except before the Godhead which inspires certain passages—the more I think of it, the more I wonder. I will think nothing impossible to man. No Parthenon, no sculpture, no picture, no architecture can be named beside this. All this is perfectly visible to me and to many,—the wonderful truth and mastery of this work, of these works,—yet for our lives could not I, or any man, or all men, produce anything comparable to one scene in Hamlet or Lear. With all my admiration of this life-like picture, set me to producing a match for it, and I should instantly depart into mouthing rhetoric.... One other fact Shakspeare presents us; that not by books are great poets made. Somewhat—and much, he unquestionably owes to his books; but you could not find in his circumstances the history of his poems. It was made without hands in his invisible world. A mightier magic than any learning, the deep logic of cause and effect he studied: its roots were cast so deep, therefore it flung out its branches so high."

Note 21.

Mr. Edwin P. Whipple, writing in Harper's Monthly in 1882, relates how in a long drive with Mr. Emerson, after a lecture, "The conversation at last drifted to contemporary actors who assumed to personate leading characters in Shakspeare's greatest plays. Had I ever seen an actor who satisfied me when he pretended to be Hamlet or Othello, Lear or Macbeth? Yes, I had seen the elder Booth in these characters. Though not perfect, he approached nearer to perfection than any other actor I knew—

"'Ah,' said Emerson, [after] the three minutes I consumed in eulogizing Booth,... 'I see you are one of the happy mortals who are capable of being carried away by an actor of Shakspeare. Now, whenever I visit the theatre to witness the performance of one of his dramas, I am carried away by the poet. I went last Tuesday to see Macready in Hamlet. I got along very well until he came to the passage:—

*"thou, dead corse, again, in complete steel,
Revisit'st thus the glimpses of the moon:"—*

and then actor, theatre, all vanished in view of that solving and dissolving imagination, which could reduce this big globe and all it inherits into mere "glimpses of the moon." The play went on, but, absorbed in this one thought of the mighty master, I paid no heed to it.'

"What specially impressed me, as Emerson was speaking, was his glance at our surroundings as he slowly uttered, 'glimpses of the moon,' for here above us was the same moon which must have given birth to Shakspeare's thought.... Afterward, in his lecture on Shakspeare, Emerson made use of the thought suggested in our ride by moonlight. He said, 'That imagination which dilates the closet he writes in to the world's dimensions, crowds it with agents in rank and order, as quickly reduces the big reality to be the "glimpses of the moon."'... In the printed lecture, there is one sentence declaring the absolute insufficiency of any actor, in any theatre, to fix attention on himself while uttering Shakspeare's words, which seems to me the most exquisite statement ever made of the magical suggestiveness of Shakspeare's expression. I have often quoted it, but it will bear quotation again and again, as the best prose sentence ever written on this side of the Atlantic: 'The recitation begins; one golden word leaps out immortal from all this painted pedantry, and sweetly torments us with invitations to its own inaccessible homes.'"

Note 22.

*The little Shakspeare in the maiden's heart
Makes Romeo of a ploughboy on his cart;
Opens the eye to Virtue's starlike meed*

And gives persuasion to a gentle deed.
"The Enchanter," Poems, Appendix.

Note 23.

And yet perhaps there is some truth in Dr. Richard Garnett's word in his *Life of Emerson:*

"Emerson is incapable of contemplating Shakspeare with the eye of a dramatic critic."

Just after Mr. Emerson settled in Concord he read with great pleasure Henry Taylor's play *Philip van Artevelde,* then recently published. He wrote in his journal for 1835:—

"I think Taylor's poem is the best light we have ever had upon the genius of Shakspeare. We have made a miracle of Shakspeare, a haze of light instead of a guiding torch, by accepting unquestioned all the tavern stories about his want of education, and total unconsciousness. The internal evidence all the time is irresistible that he was no such person. He was a man, like this Taylor, of strong sense and of great cultivation; an excellent Latin scholar, and of extensive and select reading, so as to have formed his theories of many historical characters with as much clearness as Gibbon or Niebuhr or Goethe. He wrote for intelligent persons, and wrote with intention. He had Taylor's strong good sense, and added to it his own wonderful facility of execution which aerates and sublimes all language the moment he uses it, or more truly, animates every word."

Note 24.

Lowell, in one of his essays, calls attention to the survival in New England of the type of face of the English in Queen Elizabeth's day even more than in the mother country, and also to the old English expressions, obsolete in England, but still current on New England farms.

Note 25.

Journal, 1838. *fills us with wonder the first time we approach him. We go away, and work and think, for years, and come again,—he astonishes us anew. Then, having drank deeply and saturated us with his genius, we lose sight of him for another period of years. By and by we return, and there he stands immeasurable as at first. We have grown wiser, but only that we should see him wiser than ever. He resembles a high mountain which the traveller sees in the morning, and thinks he shall quickly near it and pass it, and leave it behind. But he journeys all day till noon, till night. There still is the dim mountain close by him, having scarce altered its bearings since the morning light."*

Note 26.

And yet it seemeth not to me
That the high gods love tragedy;
For Saadi sat in the sun,
And thanks was his contrition;

And yet his runes he rightly read,
And to his folk his message sped.
"Saadi," Poems.

Note 27.

This image appears in "The Apology" in the Poems.

Note 28.

The Puritan shrinking from the form in which the great poet embodied his thought or oracles or dreams still appears in the journal of 1852, yet, contrasted to the dismal seers, Shakspeare is well-nigh pardoned his levity.

"There was never anything more excellent came from a human brain than the plays of Shakspeare, bating only that they were plays. The Greek has a real advantage of them in the degree in which his dramas had a religious office. Could the priest look him in the face without blenching?"

In 1839 Mr. Emerson had written:—

"It is in the nature of things that the highest originality must be moral. The only person who can be entirely independent of this fountain of literature and equal to it, must be a prophet in his own proper person. Shakspeare, the first literary genius of the world, leans on the Bible: his poetry supposes it. If we examine this brilliant influence, Shakspeare, as it lies in our minds, we shall find it reverent, deeply indebted to the traditional morality, in short, compared with the tone of the prophets, Secondary. On the other hand, the Prophets do not imply the existence of Shakspeare or Homer,—to no books or arts,—only to dread Ideas and emotions."

Note 29.

All through his life Mr. Emerson felt increasing thankfulness for "the Spirit of joy which Shakspeare had shed over the Universe." In 1864 he wrote:—

"When I read Shakspeare, as lately, I think the criticism and study of him to be in their infancy. The wonder grows of his long obscurity:—how could you hide the only man that ever wrote from all men who delight in reading?"

And again he wrote: "Your criticism is profane. Shakspeare by Shakspeare. The poet in his interlunation is a critic,"—that is, his worst is criticised by his best performance.

Journal, 1864. "How to say it I know not, but I know that the point of praise of Shakspeare is the pure poetic power: he is the chosen closet companion, who can, at any moment, by incessant surprises, work the miracle of mythologizing every fact of the common life; as snow, or moonlight, or the level rays of sunrise lend a momentary glow to Pump and wood-pile."

And again: 1836. "It is easy to solve the problem of individual existence. Why Milton, Shakspeare, or Canova should be there is reason enough. But why the million should exist drunk with the opium of Time and Custom does not appear."

But even Shakspeare must not be idolized. The soul must rely on itself, that is, on the universal fountain of beauty, wisdom and goodness to which it is open. So thus he draws the moral:—

1838. "The indisposition of men to go back to the source and mix with Deity is the reason of degradation and decay. Education is expended in the measurement and imitation of effects in the study of Shakspeare, for example, as itself a perfect being—instead of using Shakspeare merely as an effect of which the cause is with every scholar. Thus the college becomes idolatrous—a temple full of idols. Shakspeare will never be made by the study of Shakspeare. I know not how directions for greatness can be given, yet greatness may be inspired."

Feb. 1838. "Consider too how Shakspeare and Milton are formed. They are just such men as we all are to contemporaries, and none suspected their superiority,—but after all were dead, and a generation or two besides, it is discovered that they surpass all. Each of us then take the same moral to himself."

William Shakespeare – A Tribute in Verse

Index of Contents
To the Memory of My Beloved, the Author, Mr William Shakespeare, & What He Hath Left Us by Ben Jonson
Shakespeare by Matthew Arnold
An Epitaph On The Admirable Dramatic Poet W. Shakespeare by John Milton
Shakespeare by Henry Wadsworth Longfellow
Elegy On Mr. William Shakespeare by William Basse
Shakespeare by Vachel Lindsay
The Spirit of Shakespeare by George Meredith
To Shakespeare by Lord Alfred Douglas
To Shakespeare (I) by Frances Anne Kemble
To Shakespeare (II) by Frances Anne Kemble
To Shakespeare (III) by Frances Anne Kemble
Shakespeare and Milton by Walter Savage Landor
A Shakespeare Memorial by Alfred Austin
Shakespeare by Mathilde Blind
Shakespeare by Robert Crawford
Shakespeare by Thomas Gent
Shakespeare's Mourners by John Bannister Tabb
Shakespeare by Philip Henry Savage
Shakespeare by Lucretia Maria Davidson
Shakespeare by Frederick George Scott
Shakespeare's Kingdom by Alfred Noyes
Shakespeare 1916 by Sir Ronald Ross
Song, In Imitation of Shakspeare's by James Beattie
In A Letter To C. P. Esq. In Imitation o Shakspeare by William Cowper
Shakspeare. (An Ode For His Three-Hundredth Birthday) by Martin Farquhar Tupper
On The Site of A Mulberry-Tree; Planted By Wm. Shakspeare; Felled By The Rev. F. Gastrell by Dante Gabriel Rossetti

To The Memory of My Beloved, The Author, Mr William Shakespeare, And What He Hath Left Us by Ben Jonson

To draw no envy, Shakespeare, on thy name
Am I thus ample to thy book and fame;
While I confess thy writings to be such
As neither Man nor Muse can praise too much.

'Tis true, and all men's suffrage. But these ways
Were not the paths I meant unto thy praise;
For silliest ignorance on these may light,
Which when it sounds at best but echoes right;
Or blind affection, which doth ne'er advance
The truth, but gropes, and urges all by chance;
Or crafty malice might pretend this praise,
And think to ruin where it seemed to raise.
These are as some infamous bawd or whore
Should praise a matron. What could hurt her more?
But thou art proof against them, and indeed
Above th' ill fortune of them, or the need.
I therefore will begin: Soul of the Age!
The applause, delight, the wonder of our stage!
My Shakespeare, rise; I will not lodge thee by
Chaucer, or Spenser, or bid Beaumont lie
A little further, to make thee a room:
Thou art a monument without a tomb,
And art alive still, while thy book doth live,
And we have wits to read, and praise to give.
That I not mix thee so, my brain excuses,
I mean with great but disproportioned Muses,
For if I thought my judgement were of years,
I should commit thee surely with thy peers,
And tell how far thou didst our Lyly outshine,
Or sporting Kyd, or Marlowe's mighty line.
And though thou hadst small Latin and less Greek,
From thence to honour thee I would not seek
For names; but call forth thundering Aeschylus,
Euripides, and Sophocles to us,
Pacuvius, Accius, him of Cordova dead,
To live again, to hear thy buskin tread,
And shake a stage; or, when thy socks were on,
Leave thee alone for the comparison
Of all that insolent Greece or haughty Rome
Sent forth, or since did from their ashes come.
Triumph, my Britain, thou hast one to show
To whom all scenes of Europe homage owe.
He was not of an age, but for all time!
And all the Muses still were in their prime
When, like Apollo, he came forth to warm
Our ears, or, like a Mercury, to charm!
Nature herself was proud of his designs,
And joyed to wear the dressing of his lines!
Which were so richly spun, and woven so fit,
As, since, she will vouchsafe no other wit.
The merry Greek, tart Aristophanes,
Neat Terence, witty Plautus, now not please;
But antiquated and deserted lie,
As they were not of Nature's family.
Yet must I not give Nature all; thy art,

My gentle Shakespeare, must enjoy a part.
For though the poet's matter nature be,
His art doth give the fashion; and that he
Who casts to write a living line must sweat
(Such as thine are) and strike the second heat
Upon the Muses' anvil; turn the same,
And himself with it, that he thinks to frame,
Or for the laurel he may gain a scorn;
For a good poet's made as well as born.
And such wert thou. Look how the father's face
Lives in his issue, even so the race
Of Shakespeare's mind and manners brightly shines
In his well turned and true-filed lines:
In each of which he seems to shake a lance,
As brandished at the eyes of ignorance.
Sweet swan of Avon! what a sight it were
To see thee in our waters yet appear,
And make those flights upon the banks of Thames,
That did so take Eliza and our James!
But stay, I see thee in the hemisphere
Advanced, and made a constellation there:
Shine forth, thou Star of Poets, and with rage,
Or influence, chide or cheer the drooping stage,
Which, since thy flight from hence, hath mourned like night,
And despairs day, but for thy volume's light.

Shakespeare by Matthew Arnold

Others abide our question. Thou art free.
We ask and ask—Thou smilest and art still,
Out-topping knowledge. For the loftiest hill,
Who to the stars uncrowns his majesty,

Planting his steadfast footsteps in the sea,
Making the heaven of heavens his dwelling-place,
Spares but the cloudy border of his base
To the foil'd searching of mortality;

And thou, who didst the stars and sunbeams know,
Self-school'd, self-scann'd, self-honour'd, self-secure,
Didst tread on earth unguess'd at.—Better so!

All pains the immortal spirit must endure,
All weakness which impairs, all griefs which bow,
Find their sole speech in that victorious brow

An Epitaph On The Admirable Dramatic Poet W. Shakespeare by John Milton

What needs my Shakespeare for his honored bones
The labor of an age in piled stones?
Or that his hallowed reliques should be hid
Under a star-ypointing pyramid?
Dear son of Memory, great heir of Fame,
What need'st thou such weak witness of thy name?
Thou in our wonder and astonishment
Hast built thy self a livelong monument.
For whilst, to th' shame of slow-endeavoring art,
Thy easy numbers flow, and that each heart
Hath from the leaves of thy unvalued book
Those Delphic lines with deep impression took,
Then thou, our fancy of itself bereaving,
Dost make us marble with too much conceiving,
And so sepulchred in such pomp dost lie
That kings for such a tomb would wish to die.

Shakespeare by Henry Wadsworth Longfellow

A vision as of crowded city streets,
With human life in endless overflow;
Thunder of thoroughfares; trumpets that blow
To battle; clamor, in obscure retreats,
Of sailors landed from their anchored fleets;
Tolling of bells in turrets, and below
Voices of children, and bright flowers that throw
O'er garden-walls their intermingled sweets!
This vision comes to me when I unfold
The volume of the Poet paramount,
Whom all the Muses loved, not one alone;—
Into his hands they put the lyre of gold,
And, crowned with sacred laurel at their fount,
Placed him as Musagetes on their throne.

Elegy On Mr. William Shakespeare by William Basse

Renowned Spenser, lie a thought more nigh
To learned Chaucer, and rare Beaumont lie
A little nearer Spenser, to make room
For Shakespeare in your threefold, fourfold tomb.
To lodge all four in one bed, make a shift
Until Doomsday, for hardly will a fift
Betwixt this day and that by Fate be slain,
For whom your curtains may be drawn again.
If your precedency in death doth bar
A fourth place in your sacred sepulchre,

Under this carved marble of thine own,
Sleep, rare tragedian, Shakespeare, sleep alone;
Thy unmolested peace, unshared cave
Possess as lord, not tenant of thy grave,
That unto us and others it may be
Honour hereafter to be laid by thee.

Shakespeare by Vachel Lindsay

Would that in body and spirit Shakespeare came
Visible emperor of the deeds of Time,
With Justice still the genius of his rhyme,
Giving each man his due, each passion grace,
Impartial as the rain from Heaven's face
Or sunshine from the heaven-enthroned sun.
Sweet Swan of Avon, come to us again.
Teach us to write, and writing, to be men.

The Spirit of Shakespeare by George Meredith

Thy greatest knew thee, Mother Earth; unsoured
He knew thy sons. He probed from hell to hell
Of human passions, but of love deflowered
His wisdom was not, for he knew thee well.
Thence came the honeyed corner at his lips,
The conquering smile wherein his spirit sails
Calm as the God who the white sea-wave whips,
Yet full of speech and intershifting tales,
Close mirrors of us: thence had he the laugh
We feel is thine: broad as ten thousand beeves
At pasture! thence thy songs, that winnow chaff
From grain, bid sick Philosophy's last leaves
Whirl, if they have no response-they enforced
To fatten Earth when from her soul divorced.

To Shakespeare by Lord Alfred Douglas

Most tuneful singer, lover tenderest,
Most sad, most piteous, and most musical,
Thine is the shrine more pilgrim-worn than all
The shrines of singers; high above the rest
Thy trumpet sounds most loud, most manifest.
Yet better were it if a lonely call
Of woodland birds, a song, a madrigal,
Were all the jetsam of thy sea's unrest.

For now thy praises have become too loud
On vulgar lips, and every yelping cur
Yaps thee a paean; the whiles little men,
Not tall enough to worship in a crowd,
Spit their small wits at thee. Ah! better then
The broken shrine, the lonely worshipper.

To Shakespeare (I) by Frances Anne Kemble

If from the height of that celestial sphere
Where now thou dwell'st, spirit powerful and sweet!
Thou yet canst love the race that sojourn here,
How must thou joy, with pleasure not unmeet
For thy exalted state, to know how dear
Thy memory is held throughout the earth,
Beyond the favoured land that gave thee birth.
E'en in thy seat in Heaven, thou may'st receive
Thanks, praise, and love, and wonder ever new,
From human hearts, who in thy verse perceive
All that humanity calls good and true;
Nor dost thou for each mortal blemish grieve,
They from thy glorious works have fall'n away,
As from thy soul its outward form of clay.

To Shakespeare (II) by Frances Anne Kemble

Oft, when my lips I open to rehearse
Thy wondrous spells of wisdom and of power,
And that my voice and thy immortal verse
On listening ears and hearts I mingled pour,
I shrink dismayed—and awful doth appear
The vain presumption of my own weak deed;
Thy glorious spirit seems to mine so near,
That suddenly I tremble as I read—
Thee an invisible auditor I fear:
Oh, if it might be so, my master dear!
With what beseeching would I pray to thee,
To make me equal to my noble task,
Succour from thee, how humbly would I ask,
Thy worthiest works to utter worthily.

To Shakespeare (III) by Frances Anne Kemble

Shelter and succour such as common men

Afford the weaker partners of their fate,
Have I derived from thee—from thee, most great
And powerful genius! whose sublime control,
Still from thy grave governs each human soul,
That reads the wondrous records of thy pen.
From sordid sorrows thou hast set me free,
And turned from want's grim ways my tottering feet,
And to sad empty hours, given royally,
A labour, than all leisure far more sweet:
The daily bread, for which we humbly pray,
Thou gavest me as if I were thy child,
And still with converse noble, wise, and mild,
Charmed from despair my sinking soul away;
Shall I not bless the need, to which was given
Of all the angels in the host of heaven,
Thee, for my guardian, spirit strong and bland!
Lord of the speech of my dear native land!

Shakespeare and Milton by Walter Savage Landor

The tongue of England, that which myriads
Have spoken and will speak, were paralyz'd
Hereafter, but two mighty men stand forth
Above the flight of ages, two alone;
One crying out,
All nations spoke through me.
The other:
True; and through this trumpet burst God's word;
The fall of Angels, and the doom
First of immortal, then of mortal, Man.
Glory! be glory! not to me, to God.

A Shakespeare Memorial by Alfred Austin

Why should we lodge in marble or in bronze
Spirits more vast than earth, or sea, or sky?
Wiser the silent worshipper that cons
Their words for wisdom that will never die.
Unto the favourite of the passing hour
Erect the statue and parade the bust;
Whereon decisive Time will slowly shower
Oblivion's refuse and disdainful dust.
The Monarchs of the Mind, self-sceptred Kings,
Need no memento to transmit their name:
Throned on their thoughts and high imaginings,
They are the Lords, not sycophants of Fame.
Raise pedestals to perishable stuff:

Gods for themselves are monuments enough.

Shakespeare by Mathilde Blind

Yearning to know herself for all she was,
Her passionate clash of warring good and ill,
Her new life ever ground in Death's old mill,
With every delicate detail and en masse,—
Blind Nature strove. Lo, then it came to pass,
That Time, to work out her unconscious Will,
Once wrought the Mind which she had groped for still,
And she beheld herself as in a glass.

The world of men, unrolled before our sight,
Showed like a map, where stream and waterfall
And village-cradling vale and cloud-capped height
Stand faithfully recorded, great and small;
For Shakespeare was, and at his touch, with light
Impartial as the Sun's, revealed the All.

Shakespeare by Robert Crawford

And what think ye of Shakespeare? 'Twas not he
Of Stratford is the lord of England's lyre;
Ay, not the rustic lad, whoe'er it be,
Momentous in his doing and desire.
But little Latin and less Greek? Ah, no!
It was a teeming scholar who enwrought
The wondrous pages where the wisest go
For th' culmination of the life of thought.
No jovial actor, no mere Shakescene who
Found it so hard his dear name to indite,
The marvellous pictures of our nature drew
And limned the universe in his delight.
We do not know the man; but 'twas not Will
Whose hand is on the lyre of England still.

Shakespeare by Thomas Gent

While o'er this pageant of sublunar things
Oblivion spreads her unrelenting wings,
And sweeps adown her dark unebbing tide
Man, and his mightiest monuments of pride-
Alone, aloft, immutable, sublime,
Star-like, ensphered above the track of time,

Great SHAKSPEARE beams with undiminish'd ray.
His bright creations sacred from decay,
Like Nature's self, whose living form he drew,
Though still the same, still beautiful and new.

He came, untaught in academic bowers,
A gift to Glory from the Sylvan powers:
But what keen Sage, with all the science fraught,
By elder bards or later critics taught,
Shall count the cords of his mellifluous shell,
Span the vast fabric of his fame, and tell
By what strange arts he bade the structure rise-
On what deep site the strong foundation lies?
This, why should scholiasts labour to reveal?
We all can answer it, we all can feel,
Ten thousand sympathies, attesting, start-
For SHAKSPEARE'S Temple, is the human heart!

Lord of a throne which mortal ne'er shall share-
Despot adored! he rales and revels there.
Who but has found, where'er his track hath been,
Through life's oft shifting, multifarious scene,
Still at his side the genial Bard attend,
His loved companion, counsellor, and friend!

The Thespian Sisters nurtured in the schools
Of Greece and Rome, and long coerced by rules,
Scarce moved the inmates of their native hearth
With tiny pathos and with trivial mirth,
Till She, great muse of daring enterprise,
Delighted ENGLAND! saw her SHAKSPEARE rise!

Then, first aroused in that appointed hour,
The Tragic Muse confess'd th' inspiring power;
Sudden before the startled earth she stood,
A giant spectre, weeping tears and blood;
Guilt shrunk appall'd, Despair embraced his shroud,
And Terror shriek'd, and Pity sobb'd aloud;-
Then, first Thalia with dilated ken
And quicken'd footstep pierced the walks of men;
Then Folly blush'd, Vice fled the general hiss,
Delight met Reason with a loving kiss;
At Satire's glance Pride smooth'd his low'ring crest,
The Graces weaved the dance.-And last and best
Came Momus down in Falstaff's form to earth.
To make the world one universe of mirth!

Such Sympathies the glorious Bard endear!
Thus fair he walks in Man's diurnal sphere.
But when, upborne on bright Invention's wings.
He dares the realms of uncreated things,

Forms more divine, more dreadful, start to view,
Than ever Hades or Olympus knew.
Round the dark cauldron, terrible and fell,
The midnight Witches breathe the songs of hell;
Delighted Ariel wings his fiery way
To whirl the storm, the wheeling Orbs to stay;
Then bathes in honey-dews, and sleeps in flowers;
Meanwhile, young Oberon, girt with shadowy powers,
Pursues o'er Ocean's verge the pale cold Moon,
Or hymns her, riding in her highest noon.

Thus graced, thus glorified, shall SHAKSPEARE crave
The Sculptor's skill, the pageant of the grave?
HE needs it not-but Gratitude demands
This votive offering at his Country's hands.
Haply, e'er now, from blissful bowers on high,
From some Parnassus of the empyreal sky,
Pleased, o'er this dome the gentle Spirit bends,
Accepts the gift, and hails us as his friends-
Yet smiles, perchance, to think when envious Time
O'er Bust and Urn shall bid his ivies climb,
When Palaces and Pyramids shall fall-
HIS PAGE SHALL TRIUMPH-still surviving all-
'Till Earth itself, 'like breath upon the wind,'
Shall melt away, 'nor leave a rack behind!'

Shakespeare's Mourners by John Bannister Tabb

I saw the grave of Shakespeare in a dream,
And round about it grouped a wondrous throng,
His own majestic mourners, who belong
Forever to the Stage of Life, and seem
The rivals of reality. Supreme
Stood Hamlet, as erewhile the graves among,
Mantled in thought: and sad Ophelia sung
The same swan-dirge she chanted in the stream.
Othello, dark in destiny's eclipse,
Laid on the tomb a lily. Near him wept
Dejected Constance. Fair Cordelia's lips
Moved prayerfully the while her father slept,
And each and all, inspired of vital breath,
Kept vigil o'er the sacred spoils of death.

Shakespeare by Philip Henry Savage

Through time untimed, if truly great, a Name
Reverence compels and, that forgotten, shame.

But in the stress of living you shall scan,
Yea, touch and censure, great or small, the Man.

Shakespeare by Lucretia Maria Davidson

Shakspeare!' with all thy faults, (and few have more,)
I love thee still,' and still will con thee o'er.
Heaven, in compassion to man's erring heart,
Gave thee of virtue — then, of vice a part,
Lest we, in wonder here, should bow before thee,
Break God's commandment, worship, and adore thee:
But admiration now, and sorrow join;
His works we reverence, while we pity thine.

Shakespeare by Frederick George Scott

Unseen in the great minister dome of time,
Whose shafts are centuries, its spangled roof
The vaulted universe, our master sits,
And organ-voices like a far-off chime
Roll thro' the aisles of thought. The sunlight flits

From arch to arch, and, as he sits aloof,
Kings, heroes, priests, in concourse vast, sublime,
Glances of love and cries from battle-field,
His wizard power breathes on the living air.
Warm faces gleam and pass, child, woman, man,

In the long multitude; but he, concealed,
Our bard eludes us, vainly each face we scan,
It is not he; his features are not there;
But, being thus hid, his greatness is revealed.

Shakespeare's Kingdom by Alfred Noyes

When Shakespeare came to London
He met no shouting throngs;
He carried in his knapsack
A scroll of quiet songs.

No proud heraldic trumpet
Acclaimed him on his way;
Their court and camp have perished;
The songs live on for ay.

Nobody saw or heard them,
But, all around him there,
Spirits of light and music
Went treading the April air.

He passed like any pedlar,
Yet he had wealth untold.
The galleons of th' armada
Could not contain his gold.

The kings rode on to darkness.
In England's conquering hour,
Unseen arrived her splendour;
Unknown, her conquering power.

Shakespeare 1916 by Sir Ronald Ross

Now when the sinking Sun reeketh with blood,
And the gore-gushing vapors rent by him
Rend him and bury him: now the World is dim
As when great thunders gather for the flood,
And in the darkness men die where they stood,
And dying slay, or scatter'd limb from limb
Cease in a flash where mad-eyed cherubim
Of Death destroy them in the night and mud:
When landmarks vanish—murder is become
A glory—cowardice, conscience— and to lie,
A law—to govern, but to serve a time:—
We dying, lifting bloodied eyes and dumb,
Behold the silver star serene on high,
That is thy spirit there, O Master Mind sublime.

Song, In Imitation of Shakspeare's by James Beattie

I
Blow, blow, thou vernal gale!
Thy balm will not avail
To ease my aching breast;
Though thou the billows smooth,
Thy murmurs cannot soothe
My weary soul to rest.

II
Flow, flow, thou tuneful stream!
Infuse the easy dream
Into the peaceful soul;
But thou canst not compose

The tumult of my woes,
Though soft thy waters roll.

III
Blush, blush, ye fairest flowers!
Beauties surpassing yours
My Rosalind adorn;
Nor is the Winter's blast,
That lays your glories waste,
So killing as her scorn.

IV
Breathe, breathe, ye tender lays,
That linger down the maze
Of yonder winding grove;
O let your soft control
Bend her relenting soul
To pity and to love.

V
Fade, fade, ye flowerets fair!
Gales, fan no more the air!
Ye streams, forget to glide;
Be hush'd each vernal strain;
Since nought can soothe my pain,
Nor mitigate her pride.

In A Letter To C. P. Esq. In Imitation Of Shakspeare by William Cowper

Trust me the meed of praise, dealt thriftily
From the nice scale of judgement, honours more
Than does the lavish and o'erbearing tide
Of profuse courtesy. Not all the gems
Of India's richest soil at random spread
O'er the gay vesture of some glittering dame,
Give such alluring vantage to the person,
As the scant lustre of a few, with choice
And comely guise of ornament disposed.

Shakspeare. (An Ode For His Three-Hundredth Birthday) by Martin Farquhar Tupper

I.
Immortal! risen to thy Rest,
Immortal! throned among the Blest,
Immortal! long an heir sublime
Of realms outreaching space and time,—
How shall we dare, or hope, to raise

A fitting homage of high praise
To please thy Spirit, sphered on high
Where planets roll and comets fly?
How may not thy pure fame be marr'd
By the damp breath of earthly bard,
Presuming in his zeal too bold
To gild the bright refinèd gold?
Or how canst thou, fill'd with God's love,
And tranced among the saints above,
Endure that men should seem and be
Idolaters in praise of thee!
Forgive our love, forgive our zeal,—
We cannot guess how spirits feel;
And may our homage offered thus
Please HIM who made both thee, and us!

II.

Immortal also on this darker Earth
As in those brighter spheres,
Now will we consecrate our Shakespeare's birth,
This day three hundred years!
And so from age to age for evermore
His glory shall extend,
With men of every land the wide world o'er,
Till Time itself shall end!
For, he is our's; and well with pride and joy
England may bless her son,
The Stratford scholar and the Warwick boy
That every crown hath won!
Let others boast their wisest and their best,
To each a prize may fall;
Genius gives one apiece to all the rest,
But Shakspeare claims them all!

III.

A Homer, in majestic eloquence,
A Terence, for keen wit and stinging sense,
Brighter than Pindar in his loftiest flight,
Darker than Æschylus for deeds of night,
An Ovid, in the story-pictured page,
A Juvenal, to lash the vicious age,
Graceful as Horace and more skill'd to please,
Tender as pity-stirring Sophocles,
Free as Anacreon, as Martial neat,
Than Virgil's self more delicately sweet,—
O let those ancients bend before Thee now,
And pile their many chaplets on one brow!—
Milton was great, and of divinest song,
Spenser melodious, Chaucer rough and strong,—
The vigorous Dryden, and the classic Gray,
And awful Danté, soaring far away,

Schiller and Göethe, stirring up the strife,
And Molière, dropping laughter into life,
Burns, a full spring of nature, Hood of wit,
And Tennyson, most rare and exquisite,
To each and all belongs the laurell'd crown,
And woe to him who drags their honours down,—
Yet, Shakspeare, thou wert all these lights combined,
O manysided crystal of mankind!

IV.
The jealous Moor, the thoughtful Dane,
The witty rare fat knight,
And grand old Lear half-insane,
And fell Iago's spite,
And Romeo's love, and Tybalt's hate,
And Bolinbroke in regal state,
And he that murdered sleep,—
And ruthless Shylock's bloody bond,
And Prosper with his broken wand
Long buried fathoms deep!
Frank Juliet too,— and that soft pair
Helen and Hermia, lilies fair
As growing on one stem,
Love-crazed Ophelia, drown'd ah! drown'd,
And wanton Cleopatra, crown'd
With Egypt's diadem;
The young Miranda most admired,
Cordelia's filial heart,
Sly Beatrice with wit inspired,
And Ariel's tricksey part,
Fair Rosalind,— sweet banishèd,
And gentle Desdemona — dead!—
Ay these, all these, and crowds beside,
Heroes, jesters, courtiers, clowns,
Girls in grief, or kings in pride,
Threats and crimes, and jokes, and frowns,
Witches, fairies, ghosts, and elves,
All our fancies, all ourselves,—
O! thou hast pictured with thy pen
All phases of all hearts of men,
And in thy various page survives
The Panorama of our lives!

V.
O Paragon unthought before,
O miracle of selftaught lore,
A universe of wit and worth,
The admirable Man of earth,
There is nor thing, nor thought, nor whim,
Untouch'd and unadorn'd by him;
No theme unsung, no truth untold

Of Earth's museum, new or old:
All Nature's hidden things he saw,
Intuitive to every law;
Glancing with supernal scan
At all the knowledge spelt by man;
While, for each rule and craft of Art
He grasp'd it amply, whole and part:
Like travel-wise Ulysses well he knew
Peoples and cities, men and manners too;
With shrewd but ever charitable ken
He read, and wrote out fair, the hearts of men;
Yet, in self-knowledge vers'd, a sage outright,
His giant soul was humble in its might!
O gentle, happy, modest mind,
O genial, cheerful, frank and kind,
Not even could domestic strife
Sour the sweetness of thy life,—
But wheresoe'er thy foot might roam,
Divorced from that Xantipp'd home,
Friends ever found thee,— ay, and foes,
Cordial to these, and kind to those;
Brave, loving, patient, generous, just, and good,—
Beloved by all, our matchless Shakspeare stood!

VI.
Where are thy glorious works unknown?
Who hath not heard thy fame?
On every shore, in every zone,
The World, with glad acclaim,
Yea, from the cottage to the throne,
Hath magnified thy name!
From far Australia to Vancouver's pines,
From the High Alps to Russia's deepest mines,
From China, with her English lesson learnt,
To Chili, wailing for her daughters burnt;
There, everywhere, our Shakspeare breathes and moves
In the sweet ether of all human loves!—
Where rent America now writhes in woe,
Where Nile and Danube, Thames and Ganges flow,
Wherever England sails, and human kind
Anywhere feels in heart, and thinks in mind,
There, everywhere, our Shakspeare's voice is heard,
By him all souls are thrill'd, and cheer'd, and stirr'd;
Each passion flows or ebbs, as Shakspeare speaks,
Hate knits the brow, or terror pales the cheeks,
Love lights the eyes, or pity melts the heart,
And all men bow beneath our Poet's art!

VII.
What monument to rear,
What worthy offering?—

Nought lacks thy glory here
Of all thy sons can bring:
Long since, a twin-sphered brother spake,
How vain it were to raise
To such a Name, for Memory's sake,
Its pyramid of praise:
Our Shakspeare needs no sculptured stones,
No temple for his honoured bones!
But haply in his native street
Beside the rescued home
Hallowed by his infant feet
Whereto all pilgrims roam,
A College well might rear its head,
That Townsman's name to bear,
And brother-actors' sons he bred
To light and learning there!
And, for great London and its throngs,—
To Shakspeare of old right belongs
The Shakspeare Bridge, with Shakspeare scenes
Sculptured upon its pannell'd screens,
Colossus-like the Thames to span,
And telling every passing man
Where a poor player in his youth
Served Heaven and Earth by mimic truth,
And wrapped in Art's and Nature's robe,
Leased,— 'twas his Heritage, — the Globe!—

VIII.
Great Magician for all time,
Denizen of every clime,
Darling poet of mankind,
Master of the human mind,
Nature's very priest and king,—
Take the gifts thy children bring!
Let thy Spirit, hovering o'er
Thine earthly home and haunts of yore,
In its wisdom, wealth, and worth,
Shine upon us from above,
While thy kinsmen here on earth
Thus with pious care and love
Celebrate our Shakspeare's birth.

On The Site of A Mulberry-Tree; Planted By Wm. Shakspeare; Felled By The Rev. F. Gastrell by Dante Gabriel Rossetti

This tree, here fall'n, no common birth or death
Shared with its kind. The world's enfranchised son,
Who found the trees of Life and Knowledge one,
Here set it, frailer than his laurel-wreath.

Shall not the wretch whose hand it fell beneath
Rank also singly—the supreme unhung?
Lo! Sheppard, Turpin, pleading with black tongue
This viler thief's unsuffocated breath!
We'll search thy glossary, Shakspeare! whence almost,
And whence alone, some name shall be reveal'd
For this deaf drudge, to whom no length of ears
Sufficed to catch the music of the spheres;
Whose soul is carrion now,—too mean to yield
Some Starveling's ninth allotment of a ghost.

www.ingramcontent.com/pod-product-compliance
Lightning Source LLC
Chambersburg PA
CBHW060114050426
42448CB00010B/1863